ARTIFICIAL INTELLIGENCE BUSINESS QUESTIONS EDITION 2

JOHN LOK

Contents

Foreword

Introduction

Artificial intelligence (AI) had been one kind of new technology for human need.

This kind new technology can bring human to different benefit in global society in out future

development. It can be applied to job aspect, service aspect, health aspect, education

aspect etc. in possible. IN this book, I shall apply any cases to clear explain whether

how and why (AI) may influence our economic growth or economic recession, how any why

it will impact our traditional job nature, e.g. some occupations need to be changed or

they will lose, due to (AI) replaces? Whether it can bring labor benefit or it can bring

bring loss to labor? Also, I shall discuss whether scientists do not concern ethic or moral issues

to apply (AI) technology, what the disadvantages or bad influences , it will impact to

our next generation? Can apply (AI) technology to predict consumer behavior , such as traveler.

This book divides part one Artificial intelligence influences employment environment change and part two Artificial intelligence ethic. In part one, I shall concentrate on discuss how

(AI) influence global economic change and labor market change as well as part two , I shall

concentrate on discuss why scientists need to concern (AI) ethic or moral or immoral issues.

This book is suitable to any readers who have interest to know more effect or influence when
(AI) high technology tool can be developed to be applied to our daily life successfully in
our future one day as well as (AI) can be customer behavior prediction tool to replace manual psychological research method to predict how customer behavior change better, such as traveler behavior.

Prologue

Table of content

Chapter one Artificial intelligence influences employment environment change

Q15 Can (AI) be applied to any organization customer service department?

Q16 Can apply (AI) on education service industry aspect?

Q17 How (AI) change worker job model?

Q18 How does (AI) technology influence the future of employment change?

Q19 Can artificial intelligence impact global economy growth?

Q20 What is the relationship between (AI) and global digital economy development ?

Q21 Why will (AI) technology grow economic development ?

Q22 How can (AI) technology impact to global economic and social and psychological changes?

Q23 Will (AI) technology influence digital economy change to manufacturing industry ?

Chapter Two Artificial intelligence ethic

Q24 What is artificial intelligence potential benefits and ethical considerations? p.26-44

Q25 How can (AI) technology influence to global health care economy development?

Q26 What are the influences of Artificial intelligence and the future of defense ?

Q27 What does (AI) system immoral intention mean?

Q28 Can (AI) soldier weapon bring ethical, social and economic negative impact ?

Chapter Three AI traveler behavior prediction

Q 29 Can artificial intelligent tools predict travelling consumer behavior in airline and air agent travelling market ? p.45-60

Q30 Why is (AI) big data gathering tool better than psychological and survey methods to predict traveler individual travel choice behavior?

Q31 Can (AI) big data gather predict when climate or season will change to influence poor or better traveler behaviors?

Q32 Is (AI) traveler behavioral prediction tool similar to manual psychological prediction method to be used to predict traveler behavior more accurate?

Q 33 How (AI) bring push and pull motivation to influence any traveler who chooses where is whose preferable travelling destination ?

Q34 What is (AI) deep learning techniques to forecast travelling environment behavioral consumption?

35 Can apply (AI) big data gathering method predict senior age will be main travelling target?

Q36 IS (AI) big data gathering method a better psychological method to compare human marketing research method predict travel behavioral consumption?

Q 37 How can apply (AI) digital channel (big data gathering method) predict travelling consumer behaviors?

1

Artificial intelligence influences employment environment change

Q1 How (AI) influences labor market ?

Today, it may be challenging to predict exactly which jobs will be most immediately affected by (AI)-driven automation.

Because (AI) is not a single technology, but rather a collection of technologies that are applied to specific tasks. Some specific predictions are possible based on the current (AI) technology. For example, driving jobs and

house cleaning jobs, bank counter service jobs, telephone enquiry service operators. Restaurant cooking jobs, simple accounting record

service jobs etc. that require relatively less education to perform. Advancements in computer vision and related technologies have

made the feasibility of fully appear more likely, potentially displacing some workers in driving-dominant professions.

Seemingly similar robot, for which the operational tasks is less specific of navigating to a specific destination when following a set of given rules and preserving safety.

In the future, the effects of (AI) on the labor market in the decade ahead will continue the trend toward skill-biased change that computerization and communication innovations have driven in recent decades. Thus, some human driving occupation will be disappeared or replaced by (AI) automation driven. For example, bus drivers, light truck or delivery services drivers, heavy and tractor-trailer truck drivers, school drivers, tax drivers, travel bus drivers.

However, (AI) technology could enable some workers to focus time on other job responsibilities, boosting their productivity,
and actually raised wage growth among those still holding the reshaped jobs. For example, salespeople, who currently spend a considerable
amount of time driving could find themselves able to do other work when a car drives them from place to place, or inspectors and appraisers
could fill out paperwork, when their car drives itself. This (AI) -driven technology should make these workers more productive, with (AI) -driven
technology serving as a complement, not a substitute. New jobs will also likely be created, both in existing occupations cheaper transportation costs with lower prices and increase demand for products and all the related occupations, such as service and fulfillment, and in new occupations not currently foreseeable.

What kind of jobs will be created by (AI) technology? Predicting future job growth is extremely difficult, due to it depends on
technologies or substitute for existing today as well as they

may complement or substitute for existing human skills and jobs. However,

(AI) will also lead to substantial indirect job creation to the degree it raises productivity and wages, it may also lead to higher consumption

that would support additional jobs from high-end draft production to restaurant and retail. The future(AI) " augmented intelligence", the

technology's role is as assisting and expanding the productivity of individuals rather than replacing human work. Thus, based on the biased-

technical change framework, demand for labor will likely increase the most in the areas where humans complement (AI) automation technologies.

For example, (AI) technology , such as IBM's Watson may improve early detection of some cancers or other illnesses, but a human healthcare

professional is needed to work with patients to understand and translate patients' symptoms, inform patients of treatment options, and guide

patients through treatment plans. Shipping companies may also partner workers who pick up and deliver products over the last feet with (AI)

enabled autonomous vehicles that move workers efficiently from site to site. In such cases, (AI) augments what a human is able to do and

allows individuals to either be move effective in their specially task or to operate on a larger scale. Thus, it seems (AI) technology

will also create new jobs, raise productivities and workers' efficiencies.

Q2 How (AI) Changes office management method?

In the future, due to artificial intelligence influences to some kind of human jobs nature. So, the kind of human jobs of

management methods will also need to change to adapt the artificial intelligence technology input to their organizations. It will cause challenges for every executive and manager if who won't have effort to manage their teams how to apply artificial intelligence technology to work efficiently and easily. For example, division of labor will change among humans and machines will increase.

Thus, companies will have to adapt their training performance and talent strategies how to emphasize on work that how to make human judgment and skills and experimentation. Thus, (IA)'s greatest impact will be on administrative coordination and control tasks, such as scheduling , resource allocation.

In fact, mangers will encounter this challenges: How to apply human experience and expertise to judge critical business decisions and practices when the information available is insufficient to suggest a successful course of action? Due to this kind of work will require new skills and mindsets.

I shall indicate these change management methods to adapt (AI) technology. Such as: administration and routine tasks, scheduling , allocation of resources and reporting will fall within the intelligence machines, responsibilities that have long been reserved for humans. For example, a typical store manager

or a lead nurse at a nursing home most constantly arrange shift schedules, accounting for staff members' absences owing to illness, vacation time or sudden departures.

Thus, the managers need to learn how to arrange new division of labor within the organizations after (AI) technology had been implemented to the organization. Artificial intelligence is currently influencing into once considered exclusive to humans: assessing and acting on human emotions and personality traits. The influences to managers need to change their strategies to adapt (AI) technology implements include such as below:

Firstly, managers need to spend the bulk of their time on coordination and control tasks from intelligent system implements.

Their time spending on these major three aspects from impact of intelligent system: coordinate and control, solve problems and collaborate and

people and community , strategy and innovation three aspects. Thus (AI) will influence managers need to change their judgment method to teach

whose teams how to adapt the (AI) system operations in any organizations.

Secondly, (AI) will influence top, middle and low level management needs to change to adapt the (AI) technology operations to any owned (AI)

technology organizations in the future. Intelligent machines must be trained in context. Just like humans , on-the-job training is a requirement for

such machines because they typically arrive with only very general capabilities. To get the most from (AI), managers at all levels must participate in

the instructional experience and in the learning process and provides managers' familiarity with such systems on these aspects, e.g. How the system works and generate advice, how the system has a proven track record , how the system provides convincing explanations , how the system can make simple rule- based decisions.

Thirdly, managers need to learn how to make judgment more accurate (AI) systems assistance. Although (AI) will invariably take on more routine work and even augment human decision-making, it won't judgment work, the application of human experience and expertise to critical business decisions when the information

available is insufficient to suggest a successful course of action or reliable enough to suggest an obvious course of action. For a sense of the nature of judgment work, consider big data marketing and sales analytics. Such analytics often provide insights that can inform promotional campaigns,

including predicting which promotions will generate desired sales brand further into the future, marketing executives need use judgment, combining analytics with their own and others' insight and experience.

The application of experience and expertise to critical business decisions and practice represents the real value of human judgment.

But, when artificial intelligent machines are implemented to any organizations to assist the low, middle and top level management to make any business judgment. These forms of judgment work that managers can gather data interpretation, idea development more absolute from (AI) machine assistance. Thus, why these level management executives need to learn how to apply (AI) machines to help them to make any business judgment more accurate.

Q3 How (AI) influences organizational change?

Consequently creative and social intelligence will be in even greater demand as (AI) makes in management and the workforce.

This development will represent a long term trend in labor markets , one characterized by intensifying demand and reward for social skills

with a growing desire for creative capabilities, managers will seek to fashion of ideas and hypotheses from inside and outside of the enterprise to shape solutions to their most pressing business problems. Thus, (AI) will influence overall organizational team members who have chance to participate any decision to make more accurate business judgment.

Many managers mistakenly view judgment work as only an individual discipline, failing to appreciate that it can also involve

decide interpersonal and organizational practices. In more complex settings, judgment is typically a collective outcome of individuals'

and teams' diverse perspectives, insights and experiences. And often , the resulting choices are better informed than decisions that an

individual would have arrived at on his or her own. Thus, when any organizations apply (AI) technology to assist managers to gather data and ideas to make any judgment. In these cases, organizations can create the conditions for effective collective judgment by establishing structures , such as " shadow advisory boards" that prompt managers and employees to source and synthesize multiple perspectives.

Thus, a traditional organization (firm) might freshen its thinking is t put together a shadow advisory board, comprised of young,

digital people who can apply (AI) machine assistance to make judgment work more accurate whether related to people development,

problem-solving or strategizing and innovating for considerable degrees of creative and social intelligence.

Thus, on the one hand, (AI) technology machine augmentation and automation can give these advantages to human (organization managers) , e.g. developing people and community, solving problems and collaborating, coordinating and controlling work, shaping strategy and leading innovation. Besides, on the other hand, the next generation managers need have these individual attitude to treat intelligent machines to be as colleagues.

When, judgment is a human skill, intelligent machines can accelerate human learning that supports it, assisting in data -driven simulations,

scenarios and search and discovery activities. Focuses on judgment work, some decisions require insight beyond what data can tell them.

This is the sweet sport for human judgment, the application of experience and expertise to critical business decisions and practices.

Thus, managers will also need to find ways to learn how to use digital (AI) technologies to tap into the knowledge and judgment of partners,

customer external stakeholders and role models in other industries after the (AI) machine had been implemented to the organization.

Q4 How (AI) influences employment environment change?

Human future " micro to macro" industry trends will be affected business strategy and public policy by (AI) technology.

In the future (AI) technology will influence those six themes: productivity and growth, natural resources, labor markets, the evolution of

global financial markets, the economic impact of technology and innovation and urbanization. However, (AI) technology will bring economic

benefits of tackling gender inequality, a new global competition, Chinese innovation and digital globalization.

Nowadays, advances in robotics artificial intelligence, and machine learning are in a new age of automation, as machines match or

outperform human performance in a development to any countries. For example, automation of activities can enable businesses to improve performance by reducing errors and improving quality and speed, and in some cases achieving outcomes that go beyond human capabilities. For example, some research indicated automation could raise productivity growth globally by 0.8 to 1.4 % annually; more than 2,000 work activities across 800 occupations. When

less than 5% of all occupations can be automated using demonstrated technologies about 60% of all occupations have at least 30% of constituent

activities that could be automated. Many occupations will change that will be automated away: Activities most susceptible to automation involve physical activities, in highly structured and predictable environments, as well as the collection and processing of data. They are most prevalent in manufacturing , accommodation

and food service and retail trade and include some middle-skill jobs. For example, such as natural language processing is a key factor.

Beyond technical feasibility, the cost of technology competition with labor including skills and supply and demand dynamics, performance

benefits including and beyond labor cost savings, and social and regulatory acceptance will be affected by (AI) automation technology.

Thus, (AI) automation will impact to influence global

employment in those aspects as below:

Firstly, assuming that people are displaced by automation will find other employment. The anticipated shift in the activities in

the labor force is of a similar order as the long-term shift away from agriculture and decreases in manufacturing share of employment. Both

of manufacturing and agriculture industries which would be accompanied by the creation of new types of work not foreseen at the time.

Secondly, for business, the performance benefits of automation are relatively clear. Thus, the businessmen have opportunities for

their micro economies to benefits from the productivity growth potential and macro economies to benefit to encourage continued progress and innovation , investment and market incentives. At the same time, employers must innovate policies to help workers and institutions adapt to the impact on employment.

This will likely include rethinking education and training, income support and safety nets , as well as support for those dislocated,

when employees need to leave themselves homes to move to other cities to learn new (AI) automation works. Thus, individuals in the workplace will need to engage move comprehensively with machines as part of their everyday activities, and acquire new skills that will be in demand in the new automation age. Consequently , the scale of shifts in the labor force over many decades that automation technologies can be a

similar order to the long -term technology -enables shifts in the developed countries' workforces away from agriculture in the 21 th century.

Those shifts did not result in long-term mass unemployment because they were accompanied by the creation of new types of work not foreseen at the time. However, human will still be needed in the workforce when the total productivity gains are caused by (AI) technology.

Q5 What occupations will be influenced by (AI) technology?

In the future, scientists predict that these occupations will be influenced by (AI) technology mostly. They include : retail salespeople, food and beverage service workers, language or translation teachers, health practitioners. Since these work

activities have a more relevant occupations are made up of a range of activities with different potential for (AI) automation .

For example, a retail salesperson will spend more time interacting with customers, stocking shelves , or ringing up sales. Each of these activities is distinct and requires different capabilities to perform successfully. Thus, these job activities have similar simple control characteristics. Simple activities include greet customers, answer

questions about products and services, clean and maintain work areas, demonstrate product feature process sales and transactions.

All these activities can have similar simple activities in order to (AI) machines can be learn how to do these activities from (AI) technology .

For example, the capability perception includes sensory perception, cognitive capabilities, such as retrieving automation, recognizing known

patterns(supervised learning), logical reasoning problem solving. Thus, (AI) machine is such human, which has

feeling and emotion, such as social and emotional sensing, judgement reasoning methods,
natural language understanding and physical capabilities, such as mobility , navigation, gross motor skill, fine motor skills.

It seems that the future, (AI) human invents machines which will have these human characteristics to do human similar behavioral job duties more easily and efficiently. It implies these above human occupations will be replaced by (AI) human invention machines in the future.
Due to (AI) creation, it is possible to cause unemployment number of these above workers will increase because (AI) machines can do
their similar job behavioral activities.

Consequently, employers won't need to employ many of these skillful labor. Otherwise, they can buy less number (AI)
machines to attempt to do whose job activities more easily and efficiently. So, it seems (AI) machines will have more high work
performance to replace these occupation workers' work performance. Finally, these occupation worker unemployment number will only
increase when the (AI) machines had been invented to achieve to do their work behavioral activities absolutely success in the future.

Q6 Will (AI) technology machine labor replace human worker more or assist human worker more ?
There is no single agreed definition of a robot how outcome of a task that is completed without human intervention.
When some definitions require the task to be completed by

a physical machine moves and respond to its environment, other definitions
use the term robot in connection with tasks completed by software , without physical embodiment. However, to answer the question : Whether (AI) technology machine labor will replace human worker more or assist human worker more.

I shall indicate some examples to let readers to judge whether (AI) technology can create new jobs or reduce old jobs.

Firstly, I shall explain what (AI) function is. (AI) is a service robot that performs useful tasks for humans or equipment excluding industrial automation application . Thus, the classification of a robot into industrial robot or service robot is done according to its intended application. It is also a personal service robot or a service robot for personal used for a non commercial task, usually by lay persons . Examples are domestic servant robot, and pet exercising robot. It is also a professional service robot or a service robot for professional used for a commercial task, usually operated by a properly trained operator. Examples, are cleaning robot for public places, delivery robot in offices or hospitals,
fire-fighting robot, rehabilitation robot and surgery robot in hospitals. Thus, these functions will be future (AI) application to our daily life necessaries or business necessaries.

However, some authors agree (AI) will bring negative outcomes of automation, due to raise competeness, reduce human job nature.
Otherwise, other authors argue (AI) will bring positive

outcomes of automation, due to raise productivities, job creation, assist humans work.

On the positive outcome hand, robots can increase productivity . This is particularly important for small-to medium sized businesses

both are in developed and developing countries economies. It also enables large companies to increase their competitiveness through faster product development and

delivery. Increased use of robot is also enabling companies in high cost countries to re shore, or bring back to their domestic base parts of the supply chain that will have previously outsourced to sources of cheaper labor. Currently , the greater threat to employment is not a automation,

but an inability to remain competitive. Automation has led overall to an increase in labor demand and positive impact on wages.

The reason is that the middle-income/middle-skilled jobs have reduced as a proportion of overall contribution to employment and

earnings leading to fears of increasing income inequality, the skills range within the middle income bracket is large. Thus,

robots are driving an increase in demand for workers at the higher -skilled and with a positive impact on wages. This issue is how to enable middle-income earners in the lower-income range to unskilled or retain.

Finally, the (AI) positive impact supporter who argue the future will be robots and humans can work together.

However, on the negative outcome hand, robots can substitute labor activities, but don't replace jobs. They believe that less

than 10% of jobs are fully automatable. Increasingly , robots are used to complement and augment labor activities, the net impact on
jobs and the quality of work is positive. Automation can provide the opportunity for humans to focus on higher-skilled, higher-quality and higher-paid tasks.

Robots can improve productivity when they are applied to tasks that which perform more efficiently and to a higher and more consistent level of quality than humans. For example, increased productivity is enabling some firms, such as Whirlpool, Caterpillar and Ford Motors company in the US restructure
their supply chains, bringing back parts of the manufacturing process to the country of origin. Thus, productivity gains due to robotics and automation are important not just at the company level, but also for build industry and nation competitiveness.

I suppose that productivity can be raised. What are the impacts of robots on employment? Firstly, the main focus of development
has been on personal entertainment, which does not drive worker productivity (manufacturing production). When the internet (information
and communication technology (ICT)) innovation. This is borne and by findings that manufacturing productivity, which has been driven by
innovations in automation rather than consumer technologies, has government strongly than productivity in the services sectors of the economy in most nature economies.

It seems (AI) automation will create many jobs in internet communication entertainment game industry. For example, many young people like to use internet to play any electronic games from computer or mobile at home or outside home conveniently. Thus, (AI) automation will increase demand to be invented to any new entertainment game from internet channel. It will need to employ many (AI) entertainment game inventors to create many automation entertainment games.

Thus, (AI) automation in internet entertainment game industry will need human (AI) entertainment game inventors to invent the knowledge-based capital of (AI) automation entertainment games. The (AI) entertainment game inventors will need own research and development skills, form specific

skills, organizational know-how skills, databased knowledge, design and various forms of intellectual property to do these (AI) automation entertainment game invention occupations in the future.

International Federation Of Robotics(2016) indicated that China will be as a major robotics manufacturer and user of robots,

benefiting from jobs created by robot manufacturing and productivity gains from robot use. Chins had sold of robots to any one single market every year since 2017 year. The Chinese government has included a focus on robotics in its 10 year strategy. In order to achieve its target of

a robot density of 150 units per 10, 000 workers by 2020 year. Thus, Chinese companies will have to install around 650,000 new industrial robots between 2016 to 2020 year, 2.5 times more than installed globally in 2015 year.

Hence, China (AI) manufacturing industry will need to employ many workers . It implies (AI) manufacturing industry will create

many new occupations in China. Also, ministry of economy, trade and industry (2015) also showed that Japan currently has the largest stock

of industrial robots in operations, primarily in the automation industry. Driven by a rapidly aging population and low productivity rates,

the Japanese government has sights on a 20-fold increase in the use of robots in the non-manufacturing sector and a three-fold growth rate

of labor productivity in the service sector both by 2020 year. Thus, it also implies Japan will need many robots to be provide to service industry.

Due to robots will provide to serve any businessmen's clients. Thus, it is possible that the service workers won't be dismissed as well as

it is depended on the serving job nature to decide whether Japan's service workers can still serve to their employer when the service (AI) robots are applied to whose employers.

Consequently, it seems that (AI) can create employment, Ministry of economy, trade and industry (2015) showed that such

as China will develop the major (AI) automation manufacturing industry. The (AI) employers will need to employ many workers to manufacture

any these different kinds of (AI) robots to satisfy China or overseas individual or business buyers needs. But, (AI) can also cause

unemployment to the low skillful service workers. Such as if Japan some service businesses choose to buy any (AI) service robots to

replace their service staffs to serve their clients. It is possible that the service staffs will be dismissed, due to (AI) robots can do such as their same service job duties to achieve better service performance.

Thus, today, it is increasingly common for people to use robots in various situations at home and in retail stores, hotels and hospitals these service industries. Robots are classified into server types based on their functionality (service and utility robots or those designed to communicate with humans) and appearance (humanoid robots or mechanical robots)

. The type of robot, to which each country allocated particular importance in the advance of robotics, reflects the sense of values and preferences of its population. Thus, if the country has high population needs to use robots, then they will influence either more new jobs creation or more old job loss in the country's (AI) manufacturing or (AI) service industries both. For example, Japan respondents often associate the term " robot " with humanoid robots that can communicate with human and they have a high level of familiarity with robot. The US has the highest level of robot utilization at home and in retail stores with its people being the most enthusiastic about the future use of robots. Germany shows a strong tendency to consider robots for industrial purposes and its people feel strong effort to the presence of robots in their households.

In conclusion, to judge whether how (AI) will influence the country's employment to be better or worse. It will depend on the country home

buyers (users) or business buyers (users) how to use (AI) for their daily needs. If the country , such as US retail stores need to use (AI) ,

it will have possible to reduce some or many retail service workers. Even, if the country , such as Japan has many home users need to use (AI)

, it will not influence the employment market. Otherwise,

it will raise (AI) salespeople numbers. Even, if the country, such as Germany and

China will have many (AI) manufacturers, then it will create many (AI) manufacturing occupations for these (AI) manufactory workers.

Consequently, (AI) robots manufacturing and service needs will have positive or negative impact to any country's employment.

It will depend on the (AI) service provision and service workers' job nature as well as the manufacturing workers of (AI) knowledge level

to decide their employment chance in their country's employment market.

Q7 Can (AI) impact human job nature change?

Human need concern this question: Will artificial intelligence (AI) reduce some human jobs in order to instead of replacing machines

to do? Due to artificial intelligence is the ability of machines to do thing, that people would require intelligence. For example, artificial

intelligence machine man driving(self-driver), it (AI) machine man driving research is an attempt to discover and describe aspects of

human intelligence that can be simulated by driving machine functions. Alternatively, (AI) mathematical research may be another viewed as

an attempt to develop a mathematical theory function to describe the abilities and actions of things (natural or man-made) exhibiting

intelligent behavior and server as a design of intelligent calculation machine function.

Why do humans need artificial intelligence machines to instead of traditional human service job? For example, can artificial

intelligence machine man (self-driving) driver drive to replace human driver? I shall compare the differences between humans and computers :

The characteristics of humans are good at recognizing various things, either seen before or not, recognizing the relationship patterns between

things. Human thinking is common sense reasoning, combining all types of sensory input, acting appropriately in novel situations, learning new things and changing behavior patterns, making decisions , even when given incomplete information, working with noisy, incomplete information gathering behaviors . However, characteristics of computers are good at: The tasks humans do naturally are extremely difficult for a computer program as intelligent, which must be able to do the same kind of tack as humans do naturally.

Hence, (AI) is an combination of many different success and technologies: Linguistics - computational and socio, philosophy-logic,

philosophy of mind and of language, electronical engineering -image and speech processing, pattern recognition, robotics, machine learning,

neural networks, optimization scheduling, management information system and decision making. So, it is possible that (AI) can impact human job nature to instead of human working behavior in the future.

Q8 Why does human need artificial intelligence machines?

One of major division in (AI) is between humans who think (AI) is the only serious way of finding out how we (

human) work and human who want companies to do very smart things, independently of how we (human) work. This is the important distinction between cognitive scientists vs engineers. One of another major division in (AI) is between symbolic (AI), which represents information through symbols and their relationships. Specific Algorithms are used to process these symbols to solve problems or deduce new knowledge and connectionist. So (AI) , which represents information in network. Biological processes underlying learning, task performance and problem solving are imitated from human mind behaviors.

Q9 How does artificial intelligence influence future working changing in automation employment and productivity aspects?

In the automation changing influence aspect, as companies increasingly use robots on production lines or algorithms to
optimize their logistics manage inventory, any carry out other core business functions. Technological advances are creating
a new automation age in which ever-smarter and more flexible machines will be deployed on an ever larger scale in the marketplace.
However, researching artificial intelligence with how influences human working nature.

We need to answer these questions:

How will automation transform the workplace? What will the implications for employment? And what is likely to be its impact both on productivity in the global economy and on employment?

Advances in robotics, artificial intelligence, and machine learning are growing in a new age of automation as machines match or outperform human performance in a range of work activities, including ones requiring cognitive capabilities.

What factors are determined the changing in workplace adoption by artificial intelligence innovation? What advantages are automation?

Automation of activities can be enabled businesses to improve performance by reducing errors and improving quality and speed, and

achieving outcomes that go beyond human capabilities.

Some scientists indicated based on their scenario modeling. They estimated automation could raise producing growth globally by

0.8 to 1.4 percent annually. Almost, the activities people are paid almost $16 trillion in wages to do in global economy have the potential to be automated by adopting currently demonstrated technology. According to their analysis of more than 2,000 work activities across 800 occupations. When less than 5% of all occupations have of least 30% of activities that

could be automated. They also indicated that technical economic and social factors will determine automation. Continued

technical progress, for example, in areas such as natural language processing is a key factor beyond technical feasibility , the cost of technology, competition with labor including skills, and supply and demand dynamics, performance benefits including and beyond labor cost savings and social and regulatory acceptance will affect (

alter) the scope of automation.

Other some scientists also indicate U.S. country for example, the anticipate shift in the activities in labor force of a similar

order of magnitude as the long term sight away from agriculture and decreases in manufacturing. Share of employment in the United

States both which were achieved. So, those factors can influence why artificial intelligence technology needs.

So, it is possible that future agriculture and manufacturing both industries will apply (AI) technology manufacturer-kind of

job nature to raise productivity instead of farmers, fruit picking workers, farming transportation labours as well as factory manufacturing

workers and supervisors etc. human-kind of job nature.

Q10 Is artificial intelligence possible to replace labor ?

Not just intelligence, but also debating, if machines are capable of having a conscious minds.

Artificial intelligence has those characteristics as below:

On functionalism aspect, artificial intelligence inputs mental states, sensory inputs,

(beliefs, desires being in pain feeling) and behavioral outputs. Since mental states are identified by a functional role, which are

thoughts to be manifested in various systems. Even, perhaps computers which are physical devices with electronic substrate that inform

computations on inputs to give outputs similar to brains which are artificial intelligence composed of part any intrinsic relationship to each other. Thus, artificial intelligence activities is not the whole itself, but into parts or on external influence on the parts.

On dualism aspect, artificial intelligence is a set of views about the relationship between mind are matter. On materialism aspect, it builds the only thing that exists is matter, including consciousness. On biological naturalism aspect, it is similar a human brain than feels pains makes mental situation. So, artificial intelligence is similar biologist which might to be excited to human labor work. Hence, it seems
artificial intelligence can change (alter) or replace human labor work of nature in possible in the future.

Q11 Can (AI) technology replace human labour nature of work?

On technological innovation reason view point, the history development of artificial intelligence studying the intelligence is one of most ancient scientific discipline. The history development of artificial intelligence what aims to achieve human use to sense, learn remember and think, logic probability, decision making and calculation develop from mathematics,
instead of replacement human labor functions.

Artificial intelligence history development aim is the scientific analysis of skills in connection and practice with the appearance of computers from 1950 year beginning. The artificial intelligence (AI) can deal with the ultimate challenges.
How can (either biological or electronic) mind sense, understand and manipulate a world that is much simple and more complex than itself?
And what if would human like to construct something with such capabilities?
The general-purpose software of the early period of (AI) were only able to solve simple tasks effectively and failed

when which should be used

in a wider range or an more difficult tasks. One of the sources of difficulty was that early software had very few or mix knowledge about the

problems which handled, and activities successes by simply syntactic manipulation.

Moreover, the other difficulty was that many problems that were tried to solve by the (AI) were untreatable.

The early (AI) software whether trying step sequences based on the basic facts about the problem that should be solved, experimented

with different combinations till which found a solution. From the end the 1960 year, developing the so-called expert systems were emphasized.

These systems had (sue-based) knowledge base about the field which handled. Till to the beginning of the 1970 year, (Prolog)

the logical programming language was born, which was built in the computation realization of a version of the resolution calculus.

(Prolog) is a remarkably prevalent tool in developing expert systems (on medical, judiciary and other scopes), but natural

language parsers were implemented in this language. Then, in 1981 s, the Japanese announced the fifth generation computer system project, a 10 years plan to build an intelligent computer system that use the (Prolog) language as a machine code. Nowadays,

(AI) can be applied any industries, such as car manufacturing industry can use (AI) technological machine-men manufacture car,

instead of replacing human labors in factory. Even, in the future, using (AI) machine-men drivers can drive any private cars or

public transportation tools, instead of replacing human drivers, e.g. bus, train, tram, ferry etc. Also in the future, machine-men

can replace housewives to serve families to do housekeeping clean job , e.g. cleaning toilets, bathrooms, kitchens, even cooking functions at home. So (AI) machine-man can reduce housewives works at home. Moreover, (AI) machine man can take care old people , when who are living at homes or elder care centers.

So, it seems artificial intelligence (AI) will be possible developed to manufacture a new generation machine-man to assist (serve) families

to do any simply cleaning or cooking jobs at homes. Moreover, the overall demand of (AI) general social needs will also rise, such as security, driving transportation tools, restaurant cleaning, elder centers care service etc. So, it seems that individual or families or social needs of (AI) will be increase in the future.

Thus, it will influence macro economy growth (GDP) if there are large house family consumer group and hotel or bus or taxis or ferry etc. different business consumer

group demand any artificial intelligence machine numbers increasing. Then, the artificial intelligence products and material manufacturers must need to buy many

artificial intelligence materials to produce any kinds of artificial intelligence machines to prepare to satisfy consumer individual needs. Consequently, macro economy will grow to the owned artificial intelligence development countries, e.g. US, China, UK.

Q12 Why can artificial intelligence satisfy human job needs?

First, On machine-man satisfactory demand aspect view point, it makes computers that think, it is the automation of activities.
We associate with human thinking: like decision making, learning. It is the act of creating machine that perform function that require
intelligence when performed by people. It is the study of mental faculties through the use of computational models. It is the study of computations that make it possible to perceive, reason and act. It is a branch of computer science that is concerned with the automation of intelligent behavior. It is anything in computing service that human don't yet know how to do property.

Second, on thought aspect artificial intelligence means systems thank think like humans, systems that think rationally.

Third, on behavioral aspect, artificial intelligence systems that act like human and that systems act rationally. However,
the basic objective of (AI) is to represent human's thought processes in computation . These machines are supposed to exhibit behavior that.
It is performed by a human being, would be considered intelligent. However, some authors feel (AI) has disadvantages, such as it is not creative, it is excited in the use of sensory devices, it can't make use of a very wide context of experiences and it does not use common sense.
For speech recognition and understanding function needs example, (AI) can be applied in speech recognition and understanding function, which (AI) speech or voice recognition is a data input method. For example, the computer recognizes and understands one (or a few) word

commands.

Speech understanding on the other hand is the computer's ability to understanding a spoken language. That is , the computer understands the meaning of sentences, an paragraphs through (AI).

So, (AI) can be attempted to learn human language how to speak. It is similar to translate human language skill, instead of actual human speaking skill. Also, (AI) can assist handicap learning or language student how to listen different languages by machine-man sounds from computers more accurately.

Q13 Can apply (AI) on online shopping or digital technology industry aspect?

Online shopping can be facilitated by virtual assistants developed through (AI) technology and these assistants can offer the best advice.

(AI) online purchase coming after every product image recommendations and personalization bring important revenue to shopping online sites, like Amazon .

Smart computer graphics and games, artificial intelligence is useful in smarter computer, graphics, scene modeling , scene rendering processes in order to create, for example, effective human –robot interactions , online machine learning, online strategic games techniques etc. online computer related (AI) software.

So, online big data analysis and big data does have a critical need in the world of online intelligence machines and software in our future. In other words,

(AI) offers online technology to enable online big data analysis to provide industrial organizations with valuable information for effective decision making in short time. For example, what IBM's Watson achieved:

this machine used 200 million of structured and unstructured content with a special technology of hypothesis generation, massive evidence gathering, analysis and scoring from internet channel.

Finally, (AI) online technology another related internet invention (internet of things) (IOT) is the network of machines or objects
connected through internet. These connected objects can sense their internal and external environment, communicate with each other, can send critical data and finally can make decisions to act or correct their environment from (AI) online technology. For example, factories can monitor
and automatically change production processes, hospitals can monitor and regulate the health conditions of their patients , schools can collect data from facilities and cars can send data to car makers from (AI) online technology.

Nowadays, (AI) related industrial applications will replace most human power in fields, including call centers, customer services and air cargo transportation. (AI) technologies also help weather forecasting based on repeated rainfall pattern (data) recognition, through robotics (i.e. floor cleaning, moving lawns etc.)
transporting people and products with unmanned vehicles, sending space unmanned smart shuttles, developing robotic arms, predicting market values in stock exchanges by internet, making homes safer, helping elderly and disabled using robotic servants etc.

Among the (AI) related technologies , there are a few that significance for the impact on society and especially on digital economy .
(AI) is particularly influential in machine learning. Such as robotics, transportation, finance, health and

bioinformatics, e-commerce , e-games,
big online data gathering and internet-of-things. For example, machine e-learning is based in bioinformatics and robots that can learn new skills
for better caregiving in healthcare. What is machine e-learning? Machines can e-learn from e-data gathering, coming up generalizations and making decisions to act in certain ways from internet.

There are important applications , such as e-machine perception, electronic online natural language learning processing, online search engines, online bioinformatics, online brain –computer interface, online game playing, online robot locomotion, online advertising, online computations finances, online health monitoring, online DNA classification and decision making, online in chemistry –cheminformatics . So, online machine learning can positively
impact productivity and it can enhance information and analytical system from (AI) online channel.

What is robotics? Robotics is one of the most strongly influenced fields in (AI). For example, heavy manufacturing industries, robots and used and man power is replaced for effectiveness, precision, and accuracy, especially in respective or dangerous tasks, including welding, assembling , picking and placing . So, robots can acquire new skills or adapt the changing dynamic environment. Also, artificial intelligence can be applied in developing transportation.

For example, automated vehicles, driver assistance systems , safety systems, collision avoidance systems and public transportation. Moreover, (AI) technology
has proven to produce some of the best tools to predict stock market fluctuations from internet data gathering

method. It's predictions

are based on ever-evolving predictions algorithms and systems learn new models and make connections between historical data and new data to measure stock market trading more accurate from internet data gathering channel.

In health field, especially in health data processing , analysis, decision making support and medical diagnosis. So, online data can show which patients will need what treatment and what alternative drugs could be used more accurate from (AI) online data gathering method.

Bioinformatics is an interdisciplinary field combining statistics, (AI) online technology can help in discovering data patterns and modeling through the application of machine learning, artificial neural networks and genetic algorithms. For example, further (AI) technology development of human genome project of online data sequences.

Some scientists suggest (AI) technology is finally starting to deliver real-life business benefits. Computer power is growing significantly ,

algorithms are becoming more sophisticated and perhaps most important of all, the world is generating vast quantities of the fuel that powers (AI) technology data billions of gigabytes of it every day. Also, online firms are digital natives, such as Google online search service company is investing on (AI) technology. For new though most of the news if coming from the suppliers of (AI) technologies. And many new users are only in the experimental phase. Few products are on the market or are likely to arrive these soon to drive immediate and widespread adoption. As a result, analysts believe (AI) technology's potential will give true economic benefit in the future. (AI) industry will introduce to suppliers and users to raise economic potential of (AI) technology.

In the future, (AI) technology systems can solve business problems. Some scientists categorized those into five technology systems that are key areas of (AI)

technology development: robotics and autonomous vehicles, computer vision language virtual agents and machine learning , which is based on algorithms that learn from data without replying on rules-based programming in order to draw conclusions or direct an action.

Such as computer vision and language includes natural language processing, analytics, speech recognition technology, some are about learning from information,

such as about machine learning and others are related to acting on information, such as robotics, autonomous vehicles and virtual agents, which are computer programs that can converse with humans. Machine learning and a subfield called deep learning are artificial intelligence applications.

Q14 How to develop an estimate prediction of the economic impact (AI) technologies could have CRM activities?

It depends on gathering macroeconomic information on business revenue and the basic marketing of business revenue and the basic markup of business expenses by major functions (customer support, marketing and sales , production etc.)

An economic impact model that can gather data together and forecast the results how (AI) artificial intelligence technology brings (CRM)

customer relationship management benefits to businesses, e.g. surveys investigation includes IT spending by sample

countries, GDP and population
estimates and forecasts, revenue per employee and ratios of IT spend to GDP. Surveys (questionnaire questions) of forecast results are influenced by (AI) impact can include: results are projected from surveys and rely on estimates are made by respondents on the expected financial improvements in categories of (AI) –assisted customer relationship management activities. The forecast assumes that these estimates are correct; financial estimates are based on estimates of "first year" improvement from full (AI) implementation; forecasts are from planning to implement any artificial intelligence of customer relationship management (CRM) projects, the improvement forecast is of categories of activity , e.g. corporate marketing , digital commerce, and
customer analytics. They are not estimates of ROI for the (AI) software. They rely on conservative estimates to which each of these entities might affect company revenue, expenses or productivity. They also rely on estimates of the penetration of software in customer relationship management activities . Net new jobs created are based on the ratio of new revenue to jobs required to support that revenue . They can assume that 50% of the net new revenue will support increases in labor and the rest will go for capital and other operating expenses that may replace jobs lost to automation.

In the future, some of the ways in micro economic benefits to any organizations. (AI) technology is expected to impact CRM activities include: Spending up sales cycles, improving lead generation and qualification solving customer support problems faster (raising service quality), helping companies improve brand
campaigns and recognition, lowering costs of support calls

when increasing resolution rates, lowering the cost of recruiting employees and partners, increasing revenue from optimized product marketing, optimizing price, distribution logistics and preventing loss through fraud detection. So, micro economic benefits
view point, it seems that (AI) CRM technology can raise any companies economic benefits for care term.

Artificial intelligence enables machines or the in-build software to behave like human beings which allows these decisions and act.
The advent of (AI) is leading , talking, making decisions and act. The advent of (AI) is leading to new technologies advances and transforming
the economic and employment opportunities for humans in a positive way. (AI) related technologies can facilitate our live. For example, industrial robotics, robotic medical assistants, smart games, financial forecasting software, big data analysis, algorithms in health and bioinformatics, pilotless cargo places, drone ambulances and general purpose and workplace robots and others. (Disruptors technologies: Advances that will transform life, business and the global economy).

Artificial intelligence also known as computational intelligence is defined as " the human –like intelligence exhibited by machines or software. It is theorized that intelligence of humans can be described and intelligence machines or software can simulate it. These machines software can be reasonable ,
learn, perceive and process information, like human mind and thus facilitate human life. They can think and act for us. So, artificial intelligence is an interdisciplinary field of study including computer science, neuroscience, psychology, linguistics and philosophy.

However, (AI) research and developments have economically impacted many industries, such as robotics, telecommunications, computer applications , health, finance, heavy manufacturing, transportation, aviation, e-service and e-commerce, military , music and movie, toys and games entertainment etc. industries.

In fact, many ideas, systems and technologies have been developing in the world of (AI) technology. However, which are net called or considered (AI) products, rather which are mentioned with their specific names, such as smart graphics, machine learning, e-commerce etc. (i.e. this is called (AI) effect).

Q15 Can (AI) be applied to any organization customer service department?

Artificial intelligence(AI) comprises a set of technologies that use natural language processing, machine learning, knowledge graphs,

and other tools to answer questions, discover insights and provide recommendations. Computer systems can use (AI) hypothesize and formulate possible answers based on available evidence can be trained through the ingestion of vast amounts of content, and automatically adapt and learn from (AI) self mistakes and failures.

So, any business organizations (customer service departments) can provide efficient and effective customer relationship management of

excellent customer service quality if which applied (AI) technology system. The different type of (AI) systems include: (AI) system platforms,

machine learning (AI) based data preparation and enrichment tools, machine vision/image recognition, voice speech recognition, text analysis and natural language processing, bots , e.g. face book website and virtual digital assistance solutions, social media pattern analysis , sentiment analysis, advanced numerical analysis (e.g. IOT streaming , machine logs), supporting technologies, knowledge base dialog management, Q&A processing etc. different (AI)

technology system customer relationship management (CRM) tools.

(AI) (CRM) of activity can include these categories, such as: corporate marketing, marketing operation, field marketing, customer

support, digital commerce, customer analytics, customer influenced product or service design, product or service pricing, finance information, presentation, customer billing, inventory , logistics and fulfilment support, partner management etc. different CRM tools.

(AI) technology of CRM has been carrying on plan different stages to achieve CRM personal assistant tool for businesses. The stages are such as, in the beginning stage of (AI) projects in place, implement now, pilot phase next year in the final stage of (AI) customer relationship management tools are foreseeable future. So, this CRM technology has been improved to plan in different stages every year to prepare to achieve full capacity of CRM service quality for businesses to use in the future.

Hence, how to develop an estimate prediction of the economic impact (AI) technologies could have CRM activities, which depends on

gathering macroeconomic information on business revenue and the basic marketing of business revenue and the basic markup of business expenses by major functions (customer support, marketing and sales , production etc.)

An economic impact model that can gather data together and forecast the results how (AI) artificial intelligence technology brings (CRM) customer

relationship management benefits to businesses, e.g. surveys investigation includes IT spending by sample countries, GDP and population estimates

and forecasts, revenue per employee and ratios of IT spend to GDP. Surveys (questionnaire questions) of forecast results are influenced by

(AI) impact can include: results are projected from surveys and rely on estimates are made by respondents on the expected financial improvements in categories of (AI) –assisted customer relationship management activities. The forecast assumes that these estimates are correct; financial estimates are based on estimates of "first year" improvement from full (AI) implementation; forecasts are from planning to implement any artificial intelligence of customer relationship management (CRM) projects, the improvement forecast is of categories of activity , e.g. corporate marketing , digital Al commerce, and customer analytics. They are not estimates of ROI for the (AI) software. They rely on conservative estimates to which each of these entities might

affect company revenue, expenses or productivity. They also rely on estimates of the penetration of software in customer relationship management activities .

Net new jobs created are based on the ratio of new revenue to jobs required to support that revenue . They can assume that 50% of the net new revenue will support increases in labor and the rest will go for capital and other operating expenses that may replace jobs lost to automation.

In the future, some of the ways in micro economic benefits to any organizations. (AI) technology is expected to impact CRM activities include:

Spending up sales cycles, improving lead generation and qualification solving customer support problems faster (raising service quality), helping companies improve brand campaigns and recognition, lowering costs of support calls when increasing resolution rates, lowering the cost of recruiting employees and partners,

increasing revenue from optimized product marketing, optimizing price, distribution logistics and preventing loss through fraud detection. So, micro economic benefits view point, it seems that (AI) CRM technology can raise any companies economic benefits for care term.

Artificial intelligence enables machines or the in-build software to behave like human beings which allows these decisions and act.

The advent of (AI) is leading , talking, making decisions and act. The advent of (AI) is leading to new technologies advances and transforming

the economic and employment opportunities for humans in a positive way. (AI) related technologies can facilitate our live. For example, industrial robotics, robotic medical assistants, smart games, financial forecasting software, big data analysis, algorithms in health and bioinformatics, pilotless cargo places, drone ambulances and general purpose and workplace robots and others. (Disruptors technologies: Advances that will transform life, business and the global economy).

Artificial intelligence also known as computational intelligence is defined as " the human –like intelligence exhibited by machines or software. It is theorized that intelligence of humans can be described and intelligence machines or software can simulate it. These machines software can be

reasonable , learn, perceive and process information, like

human mind and thus facilitate human life. They can think and act for us. So, artificial intelligence is an interdisciplinary field of study including computer science, neuroscience, psychology, linguistics and philosophy.

Nowadays , (AI) is a technology almost as old as the computer industry itself, it is similar with the advent of personal assistants function

to businesses and personal promotion channel, such as (Amazon's Alexa, Apple's Siri, Google's Assistant) image recognition (face book), personalized recommendations

(Netflix , Amazon). Those innovations have been driven by a increase in processing power, lower cost hardware, and the exploding creation and availability of data. It seems, (AI) technology can impact global customer service management method.

How to forecast economic impact modeling to (AI) will affect global economy? Can human forecast business revenue growth and job creation

(or destruction) based on (AI) applied to customer relationship management (CRM) activities? In addition to the economic impact on (AI) or (CRM)

which can include an estimate of the economic impact attributable to sales forces customer base. What can economic benefits be brought to (CRM) from (AI) technology?

Artificial intelligence(AI) comprises a set of technologies that use natural language processing, machine learning, knowledge graphs, and other tools to answer questions, discover insights and provide recommendations. Computer systems can use (AI) hypothesize and formulate possible answers based on available evidence can be trained through the ingestion of vast amounts of content, and automatically adapt and learn from (AI) self mistakes and

failures. So, any business organizations (customer service departments) can provide efficient and effective customer relationship management of excellent customer service quality if which applied (AI) technology system. The different type of (AI) systems include: (AI) system platforms, machine learning (AI) based data preparation and enrichment tools, machine vision/image recognition, voice speech recognition, text analysis and natural language processing, bots , e.g. face book website
and virtual digital assistance solutions, social media pattern analysis , sentiment analysis, advanced numerical analysis (e.g. IOT streaming , machine logs), supporting technologies, knowledge base dialog management, Q&A processing etc. different (AI) technology system customer relationship management (CRM) tools.

(AI) (CRM) of activity can include these categories, such as: corporate marketing, marketing operation, field marketing, customer support, digital commerce, customer analytics, customer influenced product or service design, product or service pricing, finance information, presentation, customer billing, inventory ,
logistics and fulfilment support, partner management etc. different CRM tools.

(AI) technology of CRM has been carrying on plan different stages to achieve CRM personal assistant tool for businesses. The stages are such as, in the
beginning stage of (AI) projects in place, implement now, pilot phase next year in the final stage of (AI) customer relationship management tools are foreseeable future.

So, this CRM technology has been improved to plan in different stages every year to prepare to achieve full capacity of CRM service quality for businesses to use in the future.

Hence, how to develop an estimate prediction of the economic impact (AI) technologies could have CRM activities, which depends on gathering macroeconomic information on
usiness revenue and the basic marketing of business revenue and the basic markup of business expenses by major functions (customer support, marketing and sales , production etc.)

An economic impact model that can gather data together and forecast the results how (AI) artificial intelligence technology brings (CRM)
customer relationship management benefits to businesses, e.g. surveys investigation includes IT spending by sample countries, GDP and population estimates and forecasts, revenue per employee and ratios of IT spend to GDP. Surveys (questionnaire questions) of forecast results are influenced by (AI) impact can include:
results are projected from surveys and rely on estimates are made by respondents on the expected financial improvements in categories of (AI) –assisted customer relationship management activities. The forecast assumes that these estimates are correct; financial estimates are based on estimates of "first year" improvement
from full (AI) implementation; forecasts are from planning to implement any artificial intelligence of customer relationship management (CRM) projects, the improvement forecast is of categories of activity , e.g. corporate marketing , digit commerce, and customer analytics. They are not estimates of ROI for the (AI) software.

They rely on conservative estimates to which each of these entities might affect company revenue, expenses or productivity. They also rely on estimates of the penetration of software in customer relationship management activities . Net new jobs created are based on the ratio of new revenue to jobs required to support that revenue . They can assume that 50% of the net new revenue will support increases in labor and the rest will go for capital and other operating expenses that may replace jobs lost to automation.

In the future, some of the ways in micro economic benefits to any organizations. (AI) technology is expected to impact CRM activities

include: Spending up sales cycles, improving lead generation and qualification solving customer support problems faster (raising service quality),

helping companies improve brand campaigns and recognition, lowering costs of support calls when increasing resolution rates, lowering the cost of recruiting employees and partners, increasing revenue from optimized product marketing, optimizing price, distribution logistics and preventing loss through fraud detection.

So, micro economic benefits view point, it seems that (AI) CRM technology can raise any companies economic benefits for care term.

Artificial intelligence enables machines or the in-build software to behave like human beings which allows these decisions and act. The advent of (AI) is leading , talking, making decisions and act. The advent of (AI) is leading to new technologies advances and transforming the economic and employment opportunities

for humans in a positive way. (AI) related technologies can facilitate our live. For example, industrial robotics, robotic medical assistants, smart games, financial forecasting software, big data analysis, algorithms in health and bioinformatics, pilotless cargo places, drone ambulances and general purpose and workplace robots and others. (Disruptors technologies: Advances that will transform life, business and the global economy).

Artificial intelligence also known as computational intelligence is defined as " the human –like intelligence exhibited by machines or software. It is theorized that intelligence of humans can be described and intelligence machines or software can simulate it. These machines software can be reasonable ,
learn, perceive and process information, like human mind and thus facilitate human life. They can think and act for us. So, artificial intelligence is an interdisciplinary field of study including computer science, neuroscience, psychology, linguistics and philosophy.

However, (AI) research and developments have economically impacted many industries, such as robotics, telecommunications, computer applications , health, finance, heavy manufacturing, transportation, aviation, e-service and e-commerce, military , music and movie, toys and games entertainment etc. industries.
In fact, many ideas, systems and technologies have been developing in the world of (AI) technology. However, which are net called or considered (AI) products, rather which are mentioned with their specific names, such as smart graphics, machine learning, e-commerce etc. (i.e. this is called (AI) effect).

Q16 Can apply (AI) on education service industry aspect?

Prediction of education needs for (AI) technology student

numbers will increase, due to manufacturing industry needs many (AI) technology students in future employment market. Another (AI) technology influence if the future (AI) technological innovation, e.g. machine man manufacturing or machine man service industries will both increase demand, then with more sophistic software technologies will be disrupted labor markets by marketing workers redundant.

For publishing industry, what is striking about the case in paper book publishing industry will be unpopular? Due to the electronic book publishing industry will be popular, e.g. Amazon publish . (AI) technology can influence paper book manufacturing method which is replaced by machine man electronic book manufacturing method as well as it will cause the computerization is no longer confined to routine manufacturing tasks. Due to (AI) machine man manufacturing technology will be proper to be used to manufacture any products in short time efficiently and effectively , e.g. electronic book products. In the future, if it is fact to occur this case, such as (AI) technological machine man manufacturing method will be adopted (applied) to manufacture electronic books or any products in possible. (AI) technology will cause many manufacturing workers are unemployed. It is beneficial to employers, who can reduce to spend much wages expenditure to employ manufacturing workers, but it will cause many manufact workers loss jobs and reduce income to support whose families lives. It will cause social challenges, e.g. increasing stealing crimes if the manufacturing

workers had not other skills to find other jobs to do easily. So, manufacturers need to concern over technological unemployment which will be hardly future phenomenon if who decided to dismiss all manufacturing workers, due to

(AI) technology machine men replace to them.

Q17 How (AI) change worker job model?

In the future, (AI) technology will impact some nature of occupations to change computing. This chance will also influence some countries' economic change. For example, some factory human labors hand routine manufacturing tasks will be changed to computerization of routine manufacturing tasks by (AI) technological machine men hand manufacturing method. it will cause a structured shift in the labor market, with workers reallocating their labor supply from middle-income manufacturing to low-income service occupations.

Arguably, this is because the manual tasks of service occupations are less computerization, as who require a higher degree of flexibility and physical adaptability. So, (AI) technology will influence the human hand labor skillful occupation nature of task cheaper , such as vehicle manufacturing , ship manufacturing, computer manufacturing, steel manufacturing, television, radio etc. home electronic products of heavy machine industry change. Due to (AI) technology machine man will be proper to be used to manufacturing these electronic products when the (AI) technology innovation can develop to the mature stage. Then, any countries manufacturers will choose to use (AI) technology machine man,
instead of human hand production.

Supposing the future prices of computing are fallen, seriously, problem solving skills are becoming relatively productive, explaining the substantial employment growth in manufacturing occupations, involving cognitive tasks where skilled labor has a comparative advantage, as well as the increase education needs for (AI) technology computing of machine man subject study.

Prediction of education needs for (AI) technology student numbers will increase, due to manufacturing industry needs many (AI) technology students in future employment market. Another (AI) technology influence if the future (AI) technological innovation, e.g. machine man manufacturing or machine man service industries will both increase demand, then with

more sophistic software technologies will be disrupted labor markets by marketing workers redundant.

If (AI) technology can be innovated to produce any kinds of machine man to serve any service or manufacturing industries successfully. Then, it will bring these questions:

Can future that workers be influenced to be automation employment and productivity by (AI) technology influence? Does it impact to influence the (AI) technology countries'

productivity and growth and natural resources development and labor markets and evolution of global financial markets and economic impact of technology and innovation and

urbanization etc. issues? How will automation transform the workplace? What will be the implication for employment? What is likely to be its impact both on productivity

in the global economy and on employment?

In fact, automatic of activities can enable businesses to improve performance by reducing errors chance and improving quality and speed,

and same cases achieving outcomes that go beyond human capabilities. Some economists indicate (AI) technology would give a needed boost to economic growth

and prosperity have of the working age population in many

countries. Based on the scenario modeling, they estimate automation could raise productivity growth globally by 0.8 to 1.4 % annually. They also indicated that almost half the activities people are almost $1.6 trillion in wages to do in the global economy
have the potential to be automated adapting current demonstrates technology, according to their analysis of more than 2,000 work activities across 800 occupations.

When less than 5% of all occupations can be automated entirely using demonstrated technology, about 60% of all occupations have at least 30% of worker made
activities, that would be automated. More occupation will change to be automated. They alsto indicated for business performance benefits of automation are relatively clear, but the issues are more complicated by policy making to attract foreign investors. Beyond technical feasibility, the cost of technology, competition labor will include skills and supply and demand dynamics, performance benefits and beyond labor cost savings and social and regulatory acceptance
will affect the automation. Their predictions suggest that half of today work activities could be automated by 2055 year, but this could happen 10 to 20 years earlier or latter depending on the various factors in addition to their wider economic condition.

Over the long run intelligent machines will win against every human expert. Production robots have been replacing employees because of the (AI) technology. They work more precisely than humans and cost loss. Creative solutions like 3D printers and the self learning ability of these production robots will replace
human workers, the automatic data recording and data processing, traditional back office activities are no longer in demand. Autonomous software will collect necessary

information and will send it to the employee who needs it. Additionally, dematerialization leads to the phenomenon that traditional physical products are

becoming software. For example, CD or DVDs are being replaced by streaming services. The replacement of traditional event ticket, e-travel ticket service products or hard cash will be the next step, due to the possibility of payment by smartphone. So, (AI) technology will impact human's daily life consumption behaviors in the

future. For another example, transportation tools, such as boats and ferries and private vehicles will use sensors and navigating without human input. Taxi and truck drivers will become obsolete, the stock store applies to stock managers and postal carriers of the delivery is distributed by (AI) machine delivery method.

Q18 How does (AI) technology influence the future of employment change?

Are future nature of jobs changed to computerization from (AI) technology? Where are the probability of computing occupations from (AI) technology influence? What is expected impacts of future computing on labor market from (AI) technology influence? John Maynard Keynes's frequently cited prediction of widespread technological unemployment " du to our discovery of means of economic the use of labor outrunning the pace of which we can find new used of labor" (Keynes, 1933, p.3).

In the future, (AI) technology will impact some nature of occupations to change computing. This chance will also influence some countries' economic change. For example, some factory human labors hand routine manufacturing tasks will be changed to computerization of routine manufacturing tasks by (AI) technological machine men hand manufacturing method. it will cause a structured shift in the labor market, with workers reallocating their labor supply from middle-income manufacturing to low-income service occupations.

Arguably, this is because the manual tasks of service occupations are less computerization, as who require a higher degree of flexibility and physical adaptability. So, (AI) technology will influence the human hand labor skillful occupation nature of task cheaper , such as vehicle manufacturing , ship manufacturing, computer manufacturing, steel manufacturing, television, radio etc. home electronic products of heavy machine industry change. Due to (AI) technology machine man will be proper to be used to manufacturing these electronic products when the (AI) technology innovation can develop to the mature stage. Then, any countries manufacturers will choose to use (AI) technology machine man, instead of human hand production.

Supposing the future prices of computing are fallen, seriously, problem solving skills are becoming relatively productive,
explaining the substantial employment growth in manufacturing occupations, involving cognitive tasks where skilled labor has a comparative advantage, as well as the increase education needs for (AI) technology computing of machine man subject study.

Prediction of education needs for (AI) technology student numbers will increase, due to manufacturing industry needs many (AI) technology students in future employment market. Another (AI) technology influence if the future (AI) technological innovation, e.g. machine man manufacturing or machine man service industries
will both increase demand, then with more sophistic

software technologies will be disrupted labor markets by marketing workers redundant.

For publishing industry, what is striking about the case in paper book publishing industry will be unpopular? Due to the electronic book publishing industry will be popular, e.g. Amazon publish . (AI) technology can influence paper book manufacturing method which is replaced by machine man electronic book manufacturing method as well as it will cause the computerization is no longer confined to routine manufacturing tasks. Due to (AI) machine man manufacturing technology will be proper to be used to manufacture any products in short time efficiently and effectively , e.g. electronic book products. In the future, if it is fact to occur this case, such as

(AI) technological machine man manufacturing method will be adopted (applied) to manufacture electronic books or any products in possible. (AI) technology will cause many manufacturing workers are unemployed. It is beneficial to employers, who can reduce to spend much wages expenditure to employ manufacturing workers,

but it will cause many manufacturing workers loss jobs and reduce income to support whose families lives. It will cause social challenges, e.g. increasing stealing crimes if the manufacturing workers had not other skills to find other jobs to do easily. So, manufacturers need to concern over technological unemployment which will be hardly future phenomenon if who decided to dismiss all manufacturing workers, due to (AI) technology machine men replace to them.

If (AI) technology can be innovated to produce any kinds of machine man to serve any service or manufacturing industries successfully.

Then, it will bring these questions: Can future that workers be influenced to be automation employment and productivity by (AI) technology influence?

Does it impact to influence the (AI) technology countries' productivity and growth and natural resources development and labor markets and evolution of global financial markets and economic impact of technology and innovation and urbanization etc. issues? How will automation transform the workplace? What will be the implication for employment? What is likely to be its impact both on productivity in the global economy and on employment?

In fact, automatic of activities can enable businesses to improve performance by reducing errors chance and improving quality and speed,
and same cases achieving outcomes that go beyond human capabilities. Some economists indicate (AI) technology would give a needed boost to economic growth and
prosperity have of the working age population in many countries. Based on the scenario modeling, they estimate automation could raise productivity growth globally by 0.8 to 1.4 % annually. They also indicated that almost half the activities people are almost $1.6 trillion in wages to do in the global economy have the potential to be automated adapting current demonstrates technology, according to their analysis of more than 2,000 work activities across 800 occupations. When less than 5% of all occupations can be automated
entirely using demonstrated technology, about 60% of all occupations have at least 30% of worker made activities, that would be automated.
More occupation will change to be automated.

They also indicated for business performance benefits of automation are relatively clear, but the issues are more complicated by policy making to
attract foreign investors. Beyond technical feasibility, the cost of technology, competition labor will include skills and supply and demand dynamics, performance benefits and beyond labor cost savings and social and regulatory acceptance will affect the automation. Their predictions suggest that half of today work activities
could be automated by 2055 year, but this could happen 10 to 20 years earlier or latter depending on the various factors in addition to their wider economic condition.

Some scientists suggest (AI) technology is finally starting to deliver real-life business benefits. Computer power is growing significantly , algorithms are becoming more
sophisticated and perhaps most important of all, the world is generating vast quantities of the fuel that powers (AI) technology data billions of gigabytes of it every day. Also, online firms are digital natives, such as Google online search service company is investing on (AI) technology. For new though most of the news if coming from the suppliers of (AI) technologies. And many new users are only in the experimental phase. Few products are on the market or are likely to arrive these soon to drive immediate and
widespread adoption. As a result, analysts believe (AI) technology's potential will give true economic benefit in the future. (AI) industry will introduce to suppliers and users to raise economic potential of (AI) technology.

In the future, (AI) technology systems can solve business problems. Some scientists categorized those into five technology systems that are key areas of (AI) technology development:
robotics and autonomous vehicles, computer vision

language virtual agents and machine learning , which is based on algorithms that learn from data without replying on rules-based

programming in order to draw conclusions or direct an action. Such as computer vision and language includes natural language processing, analytics, speech recognition technology, some are about learning from information,

such as about machine learning and others are related to acting on information, such as robotics, autonomous vehicles and virtual agents, which are computer programs that can converse with humans. Machine learning and a subfield called deep learning are artificial intelligence applications.

Q19 Can artificial intelligence impact global economy growth?

Artificial intelligence (AI) is a term first defined in 1956 year. It is a branch of computer science that aims to create intelligent machines

that work and react like humans. In contrast today, 60 years later, (AI) is characterized by a number of applications, including computers playing games against humans and understanding human languages, virtual personal assistants, and robotics which involve computers seeing , hearing and reacting to sensory stimuli.

In the future, technologists predict for (AI) technology ranging from (AI) being used as a tool to aid relatively simple processes for robots with human like mental capabilities, who expect (AI) technology can emulate human performance by learning, coming to mind its own conclusions, understanding complex content,

engaging in dialog with people, enhancing human cognitive

performance or replacing humans in executing both routine and non-routine tasks. In existing industry, (AI) technology is used , such as targeted advertising and virtual used personal assistant as well as the (AI) technology that my exist in the future, such as robots with human vehicle processing capabilities.

The range of (AI) technology's progress in the future will determine the economic impact future of (AI) technology on the global economy
with more limited advances and applications (i.e. weak (AI) only) corresponding to more limited economic impacts and more substantial progress, i.e. strong (AI) technology is corresponding to more significant economic impact.

(AI) technology learning that automates analytical model, including predicting cause-and-effect relationship from biological data, identifying
new drugs, self-driving cars and protecting against fraud etc. functions. Also (AI) learning can improve natural language processing that allows computers to continue to better analyze, understand and generate language to interface with human using the natural human language, virtual personal assistant, helps users
by providing scheduling appointment, reminds organizing personal finance and finding providers of various services, machine vision allows (AI) machine man to identify object, scenes and activities in detect pedestrians and bicyclists.

We expect the economic effects of (AI) technology to include both direct GDP growth from sectors that develop or manufacture (AI) technology and indirect GDP growth through increased productivity in existing sectors that employ some from of (AI) technology. If (AI) producing sectors could grow, then

it could lead to increase revenues and employment of (AI) technological professionals within these existing firms as well as the potential creation of entirely new economic activities to any countries' societies productivity improvement in existing sectors could be realized through faster and move efficient processes
and decision making as well as increased (AI) technological knowledge and access to information available in societies easily.

In the future, if (AI) technology is an increasingly critical component of more products, it will become an integral part of necessary products of many people's lives. The extent of (AI)'s economy effort is also likely to vary from region to region, thought variation may be more dependent on the predominate economic
activity of a region and the (AI) ability can influence economic activity, rather then the economic or developmental status of the regions. (AI) technology can move accessibility and can use source development to do international business between one country and another country.

So (AI) technology has the potential to give benefits to different income chooses and to bring significant gains to both developed and developing countries. For agricultural technology, (AI) has the potential to optimize food production around the world by analyzing agricultural regions and identifying what is necessary to improve crop yield. In total, (AI) technology gives greater economic impact to any countries agricultural regions if which implemented (AI) technology to grow crop , fruit etc. food production
in the farms.

Investment in (AI) technology is such as capital investment to any countries' public or private enterprises. So, it will have large economic impact to the future . If the (AI) technology is reasonable invested to the different needs aspect by the public or private enterprises in the country. Then, it will have good economic impact to the country in the future. However, when (AI) technology is likely to affect both the productivity and employment components of economic growth in many sectors. Significant public debate has focused on projections of (AI)'s effect on the labor force.

However, for instance, some researchers have argued that the rise of (AI) technology and automation will led to significant unemployment as capital is substituted for the low skillful labor. So, they point to the concern that the increasing sophistication of (AI) technology may balance skilled and semi-skilled workers and the reduce the size of the middle class. However, this is not a new argument, due to (AI) technology negatively affecting the labor force and leading to mass unemployment. Because the (AI) technology is the substitution of machinery for human labor.

Although, employment in certain industries, has been reduced in the past due to technological advancement. For long term, the labor market has adapted to the introduction of new technology, giving rise to new jobs in new areas.

(AI) technology may also be accomplished without a reduction to total employment in the long-term to some Asia countries, such as Hong Kong and Japan. Because Hong Kong and Japan many low skilled labor, e.g. security, cleaner who complaint that employers need them to work long time hours. (abnormal working hours)

e.g. one day 12 to 15 working hour per day. Hence, if (AI) machine means invention technology success. Security or cleaning job can be worked from (AI) machine man in some hours every day in order to reduce the long time working hours cleaners or security workers, e.g. one (AI) machine man works 4 hours for cleaning or

security job, one day as well as another cleaner or security labor only needs to work 8 hours one day. So total security or cleaning employers can employ 12 hours machine cleaners or security workers and human cleaners or security workers in one day. For long term benefit, Hong Kong or Japan every security or cleaning worker does not need to work 12 hours minimum working hours one day. They won't feel tried and bore and without private with whose families, so who

will accept to do these cleaning or security jobs, even they can raise work efficient and performance when who feel happy and health.

So, (AI) technology of machine man invention can raise low skillful labor efficiency and it can help them to avoid abnormal working hours demand in some busy work life countries, such as Hong Kong and Japan. Before, one Japan female labor feel unhappy to work, due to who often needs to work abnormal working

hours for her employer and who has less sleeping and without any private time to enjoy her life with her families every day. So this abnormal working hours factor causes her to do commit suicide behavior, then she is die unlucky. So (AI) technology of machine man invention ought avoid abnormal working hours demand for employer

in any countries in the future.

The most important occurrence to any employers, some researchers had attempted to do one experiment to find that private research and development , venture capital and public research and development investment all have strong net effect or economic growth with venture capital funding further having the strongest

such effect from (AI) technology. The researchers hypothesize the venture capital investment contributes to economic growth through (AI) technology innovation and by

the capacity of an economy to use existing (AI) technology knowledge to increase productivity. They predict the impacts of venture capital, business-research and development

and public research and development can raise multi factor productivity from (AI) technology introduction.

Can (AI) technology influence the economic development to developing countries? The developing regions of the world contain most of natural resources. If one day, (AI) technology has invent one kind of machine man which can assist any gas or oil workers to seek any new oil/gas natural resource locations easily.

I believe that (AI) technology can help these natural resource exploitation countries will gain economic benefit more easily. So, (AI) driven technology can be used to change to create any new opportunities to address poor management or resources and improve human well being, such as Africa Latin America and India

can use (AI) technology machine man to seek any oil/gas natural resource countries exploitation activities to attempt to gain much economic benefits.

Could work activities in China be automated making in the nation with the world's largest automation potential? Can (AI) technology influence China economy? Could China workers be affected and jobs made up of routine work activities and predictable? Will programmable tasks be particularly impact to China employment market ?

When impact on labor market is likely to be gradual at the aggregate level, it can be sudden and dramatic at the level of specific work activities, rending some job obsolete fairly. Overall (AI) technology will raise digital skills when reducing demand for medium incomer inequality for China workers. It seems (AI) technology's effect on productivity could be crucial

to China's future economic growth as the population ages are increasing.

In China, some biggest technological companies driving significant investments in research and development. Moreover, China is one of the leading global (AI) technology development county. However, China will need to focus on building its innovation capacity. For example, United States and

United Kingdom are currently producing more influential (AI) technological research. However, if China planed to achieve (AI) technology success, it's traditional industries will need to develop technical know-how –to and overcoming implementation costs prepare to develop (AI)
. When (AI) technology is introduced into China society, China government needs to raise concerning ethical, legal, technological security etc. business questions. Also, surrounding

issues include privacy, discrimination, legal liability and regulation. It aims to encourage overseas investors to choose to invest (AI) technological industry to raise GDP growth and manufacturing industries income growth for long term in China.

If China encouraged overseas (AI) technology investment in its country. It is possible to influence China employment market to be changed. Because (AI) technology will impact to influence China people daily life. Due to (AI) technology is introduced to China society, many rich people will prefer to spend to buy any high (AI) technological products for entertainment or learning or machine man driving etc. daily necessity activities. Then it will raise

GDP growth and will raise (AI) manufacturers or related-(AI) technological manufacturers profit. It is beneficial to China because it can become one high knowledgeable and (AI) technological economical society.

But it will bring bad influences to raise unemployment chance for the low skillful labor. In labor economy aspect influence , how (AI) technology can influence China low skillful labor unemployment ratio raising. The raising low skill labor unemployment reason is because China low skillful human labors are argued or are replaced by (AI) technology creating new challenges to introduce to influence China society of simply human manufacturing job

nature to be changed to be high (AI) technology manufacturing job nature in any China factories.

Moreover, when (AI) technology introduction to China, it will cause other related social challenges in China. The varied (AI) related challenges, including the difficulty of creating safe and reliable hardware for sensing and affecting (transportation and education), the challenges of gaining public trust, a low resource comities and public safety and security, the challenges of overcoming fears or marginalizing humans in China employment and workplace and the risk of diminishing interpersonal trust because the low

skillful labors won't believe any China employers will give chance to employ them , due to (AI) technology will replace their skills and man manufacturing of productivity is much less to compare to (AI) technology manufacturing method.

Q20 What is the relationship between (AI) and global digital economy development ?

Could work activities in China be automated making in the nation with the world's largest automation potential?
Can (AI) technology influence China economy? Could China workers be affected and jobs made up of routine work activities and predictable?
Will programmable tasks be particularly impact to China employment market ?

When impact on labor market is likely to be gradual at the aggregate level,
it can be sudden and dramatic at the level of specific work activities, rending some job obsolete fairly. Overall (AI) technology will raise digital skills
when reducing demand for medium incomer inequality for China workers. It seems (AI) technology's effect on productivity could be crucial to China's future economic growth as the population ages are increasing.

In China, some biggest technological companies driving significant investments in research and development. Moreover, China is one of the leading global (AI) technology development county. However, China will need to focus on building its innovation capacity. For example, United States and United
Kingdom are currently producing more influential (AI) technological research. However, if China planed to achieve (AI) technology success, it's traditional industries will need to develop technical know-how –to and overcoming

implementation costs prepare to develop (AI) . When (AI) technology is introduced into China society, China government needs to raise concerning ethical, legal, technological security etc. business questions. Also, surrounding issues include privacy, discrimination, legal liability and regulation. It aims to encourage overseas investors to choose to invest (AI) technological industry to raise GDP growth and manufacturing industries income growth for long term in China.

If China encouraged overseas (AI) technology investment in its country. It is possible to influence China employment market to be changed. Because (AI) technology will impact to influence China people daily life. Due to (AI) technology is introduced to China society, many rich people will prefer to spend to

buy any high (AI) technological products for entertainment or learning or machine man driving etc. daily necessity activities. Then it will raise GDP growth and will raise (AI) manufacturers or related-(AI) technological manufacturers profit. It is beneficial to China because it can become one high knowledgeable and (AI)

technological economical society.

But it will bring bad influences to raise unemployment chance for the low skillful labor. In labor economy aspect influence ,

how (AI) technology can influence China low skillful labor unemployment ratio raising. The raising low skill labor unemployment reason is because China low skillful human labors are argued or are replaced by (AI) technology creating new challenges to introduce to influence China society of simply human manufacturing job nature to be changed to be high (AI) technology manufacturing job nature in any China factories.

Moreover, when (AI) technology introduction to China, it will cause other related social challenges in China. The varied (AI) related challenges, including the difficulty of creating safe
and reliable hardware for sensing and affecting (transportation and education), the challenges of gaining public trust, a low resource comities and public safety and security, the challenges of overcoming fears or marginalizing humans in China employment and workplace and the risk of diminishing interpersonal trust because
the low skillful labors won't believe any China employers will give chance to employ them , due to (AI) technology will replace their skills and man manufacturing of productivity is much less to compare to (AI) technology manufacturing method.

Q21 Why will (AI) technology grow economic development ?

Nowadays, increases in capital and labor are no longer driving the levels of economic growth, such as (AI) technology. The ability of increase in capital investment and in labor of traditional drivers of production, have no longer to be enjoyed in most developed economies ,e.g. developed country, US, UK . However, artificial intelligence has the potential to overcome the physical limitation of capital and labor to avoid missing out on this opportunity. So, policy makers and business leaders must prepare for and work toward a future with artificial intelligence. They must do with the idea that (AI) is another simply method to enhance productivity method . Rather they must see (AI) as the tool that can transform thinking about how growth is created.

Economists have always thought of new technologies are as driving growth their ability to enhancing. It can replace labor and capital factor of production. So, it brings this question: What is the factor of production (AI) technology characteristics. They key factor is to see (AI) technology as a capital-labor .

(AI) can replicate labor activities at much greater scale and speed, and to even perform some tasks began the capabilities of human. For example, by using virtual assistants , 1000 legal documents can be reviewed in a matter of days instead of taking three people six moths to complete. Some (AI) technology
may be one kind of factor of production in the future. For another example, people will work in workplace digitalization environment. So, in the future, working environment and information management are automated. Such as Konica camera sale company will use workplace digitalization. So , (AI) technology can provide workplace digitalization in order to raise productivity efficiency. (AI) technology will be one kind of production which is replaced by workplace digitalization and it will grow any organization productivity efficiently. Then, (AI) technology will assist overall social economy growth , due to productivity is raised and products can be produced in short time to prepare to sell in consumption market. So, time will be shortened to increase GDP growth fast for the development of (AI) technology countries.

Q22 How can (AI) technology impact to global economic and social and psychological changes?

What will be the development of (AI) technology and predictions concerning the future evolution? The computers and robots will develop conscious, intelligent and minds into humans, enhancing psychological and behavioral abilities and allowing for direct communication with (AI) minds. (AI) technology will be impacted human life by (AI) technology information communicative and environmental influence.

A " world brain" and " world mind", this psychological system will be enhanced and enriched the capacities of both individual

and collective cognition by (AI) technology of service industries.

(AI) technology with influence these human needs of service industries changes, such as , biological science, finance, entertainment, business, biological science, transportation, communication military etc. The personal computer evolution,

the internet and the world wide web which exploded on the scene, linking business, homes, schools, social organizations which were a completely unpredicted phenomenon to influence human life.

How can (AI) technology influence environmental protection to make benefits to farming economic growth? (AI) technology can

be applied to predict how to solve environmental pollution challenge to avoid to damage any crop or vegetable or rice or fruit etc.

food growth. Because environmental experts can gather global environmental pollution data from an environmental database to build a

perform a systematic analysis from (AI) technology. The

first step is this broad analysis can include understanding, statistical and data

gathering techniques to obtain the relevant data, the correlation among the variables involved, and a list of possible models.

The next step is to select a set of methods and models that cover all kinds of knowledge and functionalities needed for the decision making process. Once the models are selected, they must be fully implemented by means of machine learning , data mining, statistical or numerical technique. After that, those models must be integrated to build the whole EDSS. Th EDSS must be tested to check its performance, accuracy, usefulness and reliability, both from the user's and

(AI) technology/computer scientist's point of view. If these is any wrong feature in any development stage, such as model's integration, models' implementation, selection of models, database, problem analysis etc. the developers

must come back in the update th required components. When the evaluation phase is all right, the EDSS is ready to be applied to the environment. The great contribution of artificial intelligence to EDSS the integration of several methods complementing the classical statistical models/ simulation ,

statistical analysis, linear models, etc. and numerical models (control algorithms, optimization techniques etc.) .

This cooperation makes the resulting systems more reliable and powerful in coping with real world environment systems. Date interpretation has been a principal area of research in (AI) technology since the very beginning. The most demanding problem in the environmental assessment context.

Knowledge representation permits the definition of the

different types of data that the existing methods adapt to the process. There is also a lot of work to clean, repair and transform the huge available quantities of raw data. Apart from this, the availability of meta-information or background knowledge is required to guide the process.

Data mining is multi-disciplinary: It covers expert systems, data based technology, statistics, data visualization and unsupervised machine learning. These techniques operate at the level of data and background information, where numerous and often incompatible new commensurate pieces of information from disparate sources have to be brought together (K, Fedra, 1994).

So, it seems that in the future, (AI) technology with the increasing maturity in particular those related to knowledge and engineering, new dimensions can be assisted to users in environmental decision making are available. For example, many environmental systems are characterized both by incomplete models and by limited data. Hence, in the future, (AI) technology will be applied to predict climate change to reduce crop or fruit etc. food agriculture challenge by climate change bad influence.

Q23 Will (AI) technology influence digital economy change to manufacturing industry ?

To understand how the manufacturing business must adapt to prosper in the technology, we need to understand how (AI) technology will change us to shape our daily habits to satisfy our expectation of products to how we shop and even the immediate of the entire process. For example, taxi services are in the crosshairs as on demand transportation services like, available of the touch of a smart phone button expand. In fact, Yellow lab, US country , san Francisco city's largest taxi company is filing for bankruptcy as the industry starts to change faster than almost anyone expected. However, at this point,

its more than an app that is changing, some our taxi passengers renting taxi transportation to catch consumption behavior.

(AI) technology will influence digital economy for taxi passenger's individual customer experience, offering a growing renting taxi to catch of service and feedback opportunities when any one taxi passenger who chooses to use mobile phone app online tool to prepaid to rent any taxi more easily. Also in the long term, (AI) technology can influence vehicles drive themselves of behavior. Already, companies like Google and GM are working on projects to bring fleets of autonomous vehicles to cities at the path of a button. Moreover, this on-demand service model is beginning to appear across a much broader range of markets. For example , Amazon company is investing in its own fleet of trucks, planes and even drone at the same time as it pushes for same-day delivery of products. As some point, vehicles will be autonomous too. So, it seems that (AI) technique will influence any transportations choose to use digital autonomous driving technology in the future . For Amazon company case, it is not stopping of logistics. It is also aiming to automatically manage the supply of consumer home products with its recently launched Amazon replenishment service, Dash. Dash is a digital service that enables that connected derive to automatically order physical products from Amazon when supplies are running low. So, it seems (AI) technology will be applied to logistic function by digital technology method introduction in the future.

Hence autonomous vehicles will optimize industry supply chains and logistics operations through increased efficiency and flexibility.

In fact, fully automated and lean supply chains will keep reduce load sizes and inventory by leveraging smart distribution technologies and smaller

autonomous vehicles by machine man assistance. If Amazon continues to grow market share for online sales by reducing effort required by the consumer to place an order, when also contributing the almost immediate delivery of products to the doorstep. So, it will further fuel the trend toward on-demand

derive. As Amazon company fuels the on-demand economy, consumers will expect immediacy in more parts of the digital economy. On top of speed, consumers increasing expect more personalization options. So, (AI) technology will influence digital manufacturing, such as Amazon publishing to monitor every aspect

of every process in real -time and communicating

to self-optimized deep learning robotics, new methods of high volume and high customization will become possible. Then, as products merge into product platforms and even services, manufacturers have the opportunity to provide components and platforms used by smaller players. So, (AI) technology will

influence manufacturing industry to choose automated SMI lines, robots installed, automation engineers.

Another future (AI) technology development can be applied to space science aspect, such as Automation engineering space in manufacturing process to achieve digital manufacturing benefits to any businesses in the future.

Such as reducing cost, shortening manufacturing time, raising efficiency, shortening delivery products to client individual time. How can artificial intelligence give the need and advanced fast and evaluation methods benefits for space exploration?

When US NASA (space exploration organization) achieves any space exploration missions, it will answer this question:

When is it useful to have a machine use (AI) technology to achieve a decision? After all, after millions of years of space exploration and rough 10,000 years of civilization,

humans are usually quite good at making decisions in complex uncertain environments. Through, Johns Hoplains University's Applied Physical Lab. Research in (AI) technology enabled

systems, which has identified three general use cases for (AI) technology to explore space mission:

First, for some tasks (AI) technology is more cost effectiveness than human.

Second, (AI) technology is better suited than humans at solving some, but not all problems.

Third, (AI) technology allows NASA organization's space exploration mission to develop machines that ate capable of responding faster than when a

human is in the decision loop (D. Scheidt, 2012, A. Castano et. al. 2008).

So, the use of (AI) technology to enable science by observing the pace of rapidly evolving phenomena was demonstrated. It is more effectively coordinating and

(AI) technology utilizing to earn economic benefits to use for space exploration mission.

However, (AI) technology also have current risk for space

exploration. Today (AI) technology is immature and requires further development to reach its potential. For instance, the (AI) technology algorithms that detected the dust derive could not have identified whether the Martain weather represented a threat to the cover. Also it can not yet use instrument input to determine what, where and how to autonomously make the next space science measurement. An equally important factor limiting

(AI)'s deployment is that lacks the methodology and technology to effectively test (AI) technology. So, the challenge will testing (AI) enabled system is how (AI) performance can be measured. It would be NASA organization's difficulty to find (AI) technology to develop to carry on researching any space exploration missions in the

future. However, (AI) technology will be a good economic benefit choice for space exploration mission in the future.

2

Artificial intelligence ethic

—♥—

Q24 What is artificial intelligence potential benefits and ethical considerations?

The ability of (AI) technology systems to transform vast amounts of complex information into insight has the potential to help solve
manufacturing or service challenges for human needs. However, to reap the societal benefits of (AI) systems, humans will need to trust then and make sure that which follow the same ethical principles, moral values, professional codes and social norms that we humans would follow in the same scenario, research
and educational efforts as well as carefully designed regulation in order to achieve the most effort of economic benefits goals. For example, international business machines corporation (IBM) is actively engaged both competitors , in global discussions about how to make (AI) ethical and as beneficial as possible for people as social economic benefits.

(AI) is usually defined as the " capability of a computer program to perform tasks or reasoning processes " that human usually associate to intelligence in a human being. Often, it has to do with the ability to make a good decision, even when there is uncertainty,
too much information to handle. As an example, play chess or complex card games of entertainment activities is believed to need some form of intelligence in a human being, as well as choosing the best medical facilities in a difficult medical case, or creating something new, such as mathematical theorem or even some
form of act, or even driving automatic machine man (self driving vehicle) replacing human driving in the middle of a crowded city.

(AI) needs depends on what we consider being intelligence in the behavior of a human being act a certain point in time. If human belief about human intelligence changes and we don't believe any longer that a certain task requires intelligence, then a computer program performing that task is no longer part of (AI), it becomes just another boring computer program. So, it means that (AI) technology will replace some old computer programs, if human
can invent new generation of (AI) software for any functions or activities to satisfy human needs.

As IBM, it argues intelligence. This means that we aim to build systems that enhance and scale human expertise and skills rather than replacing them. We therefore focus on practical applications of (AI) capabilities that assist people in performing well-defined tasks of needs by exploiting and wide range of (AI)-based services.
We also use the term " cognitive computing" it is mean a comprehensive net of capabilities based on technology. It comprises the fields of machine learning, reasoning and

decision technologies, language, speech and vision recognition and processing technologies, high performance and high efficient functions for any industries or individual consumers needs. For example, robotics, which are usually very good at doing what which are supposed to in any environment, much have public shopping center, factory etc.

places which need simply services from the robot (machine man), such as cleans the floor of our houses to the robot that can work together with humans in production chains, passing through the warehouse, robots can take care of the tasks of an entire warehouse and the companion robots like Nao, Pepper, Aibo and Giraff, who can entertain use, talk to use and help elderly people to stay connected to their friends, relatives and doctors.

Google company is building automatic machine (self-driving cars) and has acquired more than 10 robotics companies. Facebook had opened whole new research facility only on (AI) research. Apply computer has developed Siri. Microsoft computer company has built a similar personalized assistant. Google

has Deep mind, a UK company whose long term aim is to build general (AI) and has already great potential to win game to the world champion and IBM is investing a huge amount of resources in applying its Watson cognitive computing system to the medical domains to finance and to personalized education. In Europe, IBM is establishing new centers in Munich and Milan focused in the application of cognitive computer capabilities to the internet of things and healthcare respectively. For example, automatic machine man (self-driving cars) are all about (AI), which used to be able to see what happens in the street (signals ,lanes, other cars, pedestrians, traffic lights, which need to

able predict
what other cars and pedestrians will do, and who need to
be able to cope with unforeseen situations. Since, most car
accidents are due to human fault, it is estimated that the
adoption
of self-driving cars will save about half of the lives that are
usually last in car accidents.

IBM Watson company has to understand spoken language,
make sense of massive amount to text , respond correctly to
questions in many categories, as well as assess its
own confidence in responding to such questions. In the
future, (AI) technology can own question/answering
capabilities that would be very useful, for example, in
assisting a doctor
when trying to some to the correct diagnosis for a patient
and to propose the best therapy .

Intelligent machines can also rely on huge amounts of
data to be used to learn how to make better decisions. This
data comes from all of us over the years Facebook users
have uploaded more than 250 billion pictures and every
day who upload about 350 million more. Every second, we
submit 40,000 google search queries. So, (AI)
technology will be connected through the web from
appliances to traffic lights from cars to watches. Other tasks
that are very easy for humans are physical and
manipulation
tasks, such as walking , running, picking up an object to
make its shape and location, restricted environment. But
(AI) machine man technology still not able to have the
general physical and manipulation capabilities even of a 6
year old.

So, it brings this question: Why do (AI) scientists need to concern ethics? Because (AI) technology is complex, information into insight has the potential to reveal long held secrets and help solve some of the world's most difficult problems. (AI) systems can potentially be used to help discover insights to treat disease,

predict the whether, and manage the global economy. So, ethic issues is important to and (AI) scientists . If any one new (AI) technology research investigation could success, it will be a secret to and the (AI) scientists can not permit to their loyalty to any competitors to damage the fair (AI) technology products trading market.

The country (countries) (AI) technology scientists need to concern ethic issues, who need to keep secrets for their countries economic or/and social benefits. This is moral issues to any countries/country loyalty is whose countries intangible assets. They can not sell (AI) loyalty to any their countries to assist whose

economic benefits immorally.

Q25 How can (AI) technology influence to global health care economy development?

According to (AI) lecturer analysis, when combined key clinical health (AI) application can potentially create $150 billion in annual savings for the US healthcare economy by 2026 year. (AI) technology is re-winning modern conception of healthcare delivery. It enables machines to sense, comprehend, act and learn. So which can perform administrative and clinical healthcare functions (Accenture, 2017).

It will help health care service organizations to reduce health care cost, will improve and raise service quality and access. So, (AI) health market size will be predicted growth. (AI) applications in health care include robot-assisted surgery, virtual nursing an assistant, administrative workflow assistant, fraud detection, error reduction connected machines, clinical trial participant identifier, preliminary diagnosis, automated image diagnosis and cybersecurity.

What kind of benefits (AI) technology can contribute to healthcare service? (AI) technology can deliver what many health care organizations need, such as financial and operational of labor costs, digital expectations from patient consumers how to use (AI) technology to solve interoperability challenges

in any healthcare organizations. Also (AI) technology can be applied to wellness an d lifestyle management, diagnostics, delivers financially but also way of

organizational and workflow improvement. So, (AI) technology will be continue to become most prevalent and adoption to healthcare organizations , which must need to enhance structure to be position to take full advantages of new (AI) technological capabilities. (AI) technology can change the nature of work and employment is rapidly changing to make the best use of both humans and (AI) talent in healthcare industry in the future. For example, (AI) technology offers a way to fill in gaps and the rising labor shortage in healthcare. According to Accentuare analysis, the

physicians shortage is increasing. However, (AI) technology will manufacture healthcare machine men to replace physicians in future one day(2017).

Hence, (AI) technology will be invented to raise health care service staffs work efficiency and performance in any hospitals or clinics in the future.

In conclusion, (AI) technology will raise efficiency for any service or manufacturing industries in the future, although, it is possible that it will also rise low skillful workers unemployment numbers. But, the most important influence to human technological innovation will be risen and it will influence human life will be changed to be better, e.g. self drive cars, health care physician machine men, machine man cleaners etc. intelligent machine men will be manufactured to serve for our daily life. Furthermore, (AI) technological products will influence countries trading, some low technological

development countries manufacturing businessmen can choose to buy any (AI) products to raise whose productivity and efficiency and reducing cost to achieve economic cost saving result. Also, GDP of trading growth income will increase to the (AI) products sale countries. Hence, it will be beneficial to economic

development to both developed and developing countries both in the future as well as (AI) scientists ti and money spending will be valued to continue to invest

(AI) technology development for human life and economy benefits for long term.

In conclusion (AI) technology will raise macro economy growth and it can create many (AI) jobs , but it also raise the low level technological worker unemployment change. In the future, (AI) technology can be applied to digital technology to attempt to invent any new undiscovered (AI) and digital technology. So, it needs any scientists to continue to research how digital and (AI) technology can be mixed to satisfy human's future undiscovered needs.

Q26 What are the influences of Artificial intelligence and the future of defense ?

Nowadays, artificial intelligence (AI) is widely knowledge to be one kind of the dramatic technology. However, it is expected to continue,

to have a disruptive impact on human's private and public life, so defense and security will be no exception. But how exactly will these be affected ?

How will (AI) defense and security is incremental in nature?

To research why artificial intelligence (AI) has possible to be used to cause autonomous weapons by human. We need to understand these

three aspects of relationship. They include cybersecurity and artificial intelligence and machine learning and autonomous weapon systems relationship between of them.

Firstly, we need to know what is the mean of artificial intelligence and cyber defense/offense? It means defense of critical networks: real time,

Pattern finding, anomaly seeking, it must utilize machine (AI) learning algorithms to efficiently, and instantaneously respond to potential network threats as well as it means human on or out of the loop. On the loop : it means anomaly detection: human notified, IT analysis, response. Out of the loop: it means anomaly detection:

(AI) decides best method of response: quarantine, honey pot monitoring, hack-back. Thus, it is possible that (AI) can be used , such as autonomous cyber weapon.

What is artificial intelligence and autonomous weapons? Autonomous weapons mean one kind of weapon that can be selected

and engaged a target, without intervention by a human

operator. Are these machines artificially intelligent? I believe the answer is not,

because present weapons systems are not capable of human level reasoning. But, (AI) algorithms are presently employed to process sensor data,

monitor system health, take and respond to vocal commands manage data, navigate. This, future autonomous weapons systems will require stronger (AI) to be secure and operationally and cost effective. Moreover, self-aware autonomous cyber systems are crucial.

What is cybersecurity mean? It means the ability to control access to networked systems and the information they contain.

It is acted to prevent , detect, recover, react. It is application objects concern people, process, technology and it's application goals are confidentiality, integrity and popular availability. Thus, what is cyber weapon mean? Walware means viruses, Trojans, zero-days, worms ransomware, spyware etc. Does it require

a particular objective? E.g. military paramilitary or intelligence. Does it require physical harm? E.g. functional harm or interruption? Mental harm? Is

(AI) a technological weapon that it is an object or tool? What about when it is an weapon agent?

In simplicity, (AI) can be one of scientific weapons platform. When one day, it is invented to be applied to control war planes to

fly to any countries to attack enemies or it is invented to be seemed to human to replace soldiers to bring guns or any weapons go to other countries to attack. So, it is possible that future any war defense planes, (AI) technological automatic control weapon can be replaced of human soldiers or war plane pilots to control any war defense planes to go to different enemy countries to attack them easily. It is very horror matter to threaten global human's ourselves life in the future , if (AI) automatic control war defense planes or (AI) automatic control machine soldiers were invented successfully.

Hence , when (AI) can be applied to weapons platforms, it structures that launch weapons, i.e. jets, ships, vehicles. (AI) platform and weapon and

software architecture components are be done one (AI) technological weapons systems. Thus, human will encounter any (AI) benefits or risks (threats) causes in the same time as soon as possible. If we can predict when (AI) weapon system will be manufactured or invented successfully. Then, we can reduce (AI) weapon

systems risks , if we can threaten any (AI) scientists continue to invent any undiscovered (AI) weapons in any time to avoid the future first time (AI) weapon war occurrence in possible.

The (AI) weapon system risk means autonomy: the ability to problem solve technological war , when (AI) weapon system is manufactured successfully, the power to act, how to damage the (AI) weapon system. The power to chance to stop (AI) weapon system manufacturing processes, ability to create a new goals,

how to change the (AI) weapon system inventors' or scientists' minds to avoid to apply (AI) tools to achieve attack goals to change to another positive goal. Due to human can't know a prior what an autonomous (AI) weapon system will do.

Although, human is known what (AI) is , but human is also known when (AI) scientists whose emergent behaviors will do to change to do any negative behaviors from positive behaviors. Whatever (AI) weapon system design we use, there will be cybersecurity, problems arising from computation design/complexity. Due to any one

(AI) scientist can manipulate the system to act against itself, or who can utilize traditional " cyber weapons" against the (AI) weapon system, or who can manipulate the system to lie to humans, but also due to complexity, there is no way to know if it is lying or not or bounded rationality : satisficing.

Finally, the most serious (AI) technological invention risks are human is unknown these aspects of (AI) absolutely: They are not simple automatic systems, learning reasoning, communication of " self-aware" systems. Thus, human will face (AI) technological invention risks or threats. We need to find any methods to avoid

(AI) weapon system is manufactured successfully to avoid (AI) technological war can occur in future anyone day.

Q27 What does (AI) system immoral intention mean?

Why (AI) system can be invented to damage our society ? IS it possible to achieve this (AI) damage system successfully?

ON (AI) attribution hand, it can be applied to cars, aircraft, which are subject to regulation designed to protect the public from harm and

ensure fairness in economic competition. Thus, (AI) safety issue is important to scientists to consider.

IN general, the approach to regulation of (AI)-enabled products protect public safety issue should be informed by assessment of the

aspects of risk that the addition of (AI) way reduce any respects of risk that it may increase. Also, where regulatory responses to the addition of

(AI) threaten to increase the cost of compliance, or slow the development or adoption of beneficial innovations, policymakers should consider how those responses could be adjusted to lower costs and barriers to innovation without adversely impacting safety or market fairness.

For example, regulatory challenges that (AI) enabled present are found in the cases of automated vehicles. (AI)s, such as self-driving cars and (AI)-equipped unmanned aircraft systems. IN the long run, self-driving cars will likely save many lives by reducing driver error and increasing personal mobility, it will offer many economic benefits. Thus, public safety must be protected as these technologies are tested and begin to mature. Creating safe spaces and test beds for experimentation , and working with industry and civil society to evolve performance based regulations that will enable more uses as

evidence of safe operation accumulates. Thus, it implies that any scientists can also invent (AI) system to control weapon defense planes or (AI)

automatic machine human to do any soldier's behaviors to attack to any countries easily, instead of none driver automatic control vehicle invention.

Thus, (AI) system can be applied to harm to human or achieve to damage our society aim by ourselves in possible.

The rapid growth of (AI) has dramatically increased the need for people with relevant skills to support and advance the field. AN (AI) –enables

would demand a data literate citizenry that is able to read, use, interpret and communicate about data and participate in policy debates about matters affected by (AI).

Thus, if (AI) technology is applied to assist human's social development and raising life enjoyment or benefits. It will bring positive impact to influence human's future life. Otherwise, if (AI) technology is unsafe to be applied to threaten human's society. It will bring negative impact to influence human's future life. Thus, (AI) scientists need to consider how to apply (AI) technology.

As (AI) technologies move toward deployment, technical expects, policy analysts and ethicists have raised concerns about unintended, consequences of adoption.
Use one (AI) to make consequential decisions about people, often replacing decisions made by human –driven bureaucratic processes, leads to concerns about how to ensure
justice, fairness, and accountability, the same concerns of human's safety issue. Thus,)AI) expects have cautioned that there are challenges in trying to understand and predict the behaviors of advanced (AI) systems.

Use of (AI) to control physical-world equipment leads to concerns about safety, especially as systems are exposed to the full complexity of human environment.
A major challenge in (AI) safety is building systems that can safety transition from the closed world of the laboratory into the outside open world, when unpredictable things can happen. Adapting to unforeseen situations are difficult necessary for safe operation. Experience in building other types of safety artificial systems and, such
as aircraft, power plants, bridges and vehicles has much to teach (AI) practitioners about verification and validation, how to build a safety case for a technology, how to manage risks, and how to communicate with stakeholders about risk. The risk means the harm of human's safety of (AI) damage system control machine invention. Thus, any (AI) scientists need consider moral responsibility when who decide to invent what kind of (AI) system machine to aim to bring human's benefits or attribute to human's welfare intention.

Thus, (AI) products safe invention matter will need any scientists' considerations. Because , if (AI) any products are unsafe or harm human's invention in the manufacturing process, it will bring any human's life danger when the (AI) system damage tools are invented successfully and are provided weapons to humans to use to attack
other countries easily. It will cause future global human (AI) technological war occurrence.

I shall recommend the solution is necessary of ethical training for (AI) practitioners and students. Ideally, every student learning (AI) , computer science, or data science would be exposed to curriculum and discussion on related ethics and security topics. However, ethics alone is not sufficient. Ethics can help practitioners
understand their responsibilities to all stakeholders, but ethical training should be methods for deciding good intentions into practice by doing the technical work needed to prevent unacceptable or immoral (AI) invention outcomes.

Hence, global human needs to concern (AI) weapon system invention security issue. Nowadays, (AI) has important application is increasing role for both defensive and
offensive cyber measures. Currently, designing and operating secure systems requires significant time and attention from experts.

Challenges issues are raised by the potential use of (AI) in weapon systems. The United States has incorporated autonomy in certain weapon systems for decades, allowing for greater precision in the use of weapons and safer, more humane military operations. Nonetheless, direct human control of weapon systems involves some risks
and can raise legal and ethical questions concern (AI)

manufacturing process intention.

The key to incorporating autonomous and semi-autonomous weapon system into American defense planning is to ensure that U.S. Government entities are always acting

in accordance with international humanitarian law, taking appropriate steps to control , to develop standards related to the development and use of such weapon systems.

The United States has activity participated in ongoing international discussion on Lethal autonomous weapon systems and anticipates continued robust international discussion

of those potential weapons systems. Thus, (AI) scientists have responsibilities to manage the potential to be a major driver of economic growth and social progress only, their

(AI) intentions are not the global dominance aims absolutely, if (AI) product industry , civil society, government and the public work together to support (AI) positive development

of the technology with thoughtful attention to its potential and to managing its invention threat risks to avoid (AI) products to manufacture to be used weapon tools.

Finally, I recommend that as the technology of (AI) continues to develop, practitioners must ensure that (AI) enables systems are governable, that what their inventions need to be openness to let public to know clearly and understandable; that they can work effectively with people and that their operation will remain consistent with human values and

aspirations. Researchers and practitioners have increased their attention to these challenges , and should continue to focus on their future any (AI) inventions.

Hence, (AI) safe system ought to be applied to solve the biggest challenges that society faces, such as mobility for the elderly and those with disabilities, smart buildings
may save energy and reduce carbon emissions, precision medicine may extend life and increase quality of life, smarter government may solve citizens more quickly and precisely.,
better protect those at any immoral invention risk and save money.

Moreover, (AI) enhanced education may help teachers give every child on education that opens doors to a secure and fulfilling life. Thus, these are the future human's potential benefits if the (AI) technology is developed to its benefits and scientists ought avoid to manufacture (AI) tools to cause weapon risks and challenges.

Consequently, the main point is that how experts invent (AI) systems. (AI) systems ought not be advanced weapon systems, it doesn't seem to be thought similar human soldiers mind and behaviors. (AI) system ought be systems that think like humans. (e.g. cognitive architectures and neural networks), systems that act like humans
(e.g. pass the test via natural language process, knowledge representation, automated reasoning, and learning), systems that think rationally , e.g. logic solvers, inference and optimization and systems that act rationally e.g. intelligence software agents and embodies robots that achieve goals via perception, planning reasoning, learning , communicating, decision-making and acting function.

In conclusion, it is horror (AI) scientists will invent (AI) systems to be owned human's (soldier's) mind and attack strategic behavior to attack other countries easily, who must need to consider (AI) system ought be invented to own scientists' creating mind and non manual assistance functions for positive attribution to human's society. I expect that (AI) system can only be invented to create human's welfare in our future.

Q28 Can (AI) soldier weapon bring ethical, social and economic negative impact ?

In the future, how human can avoid (AI) technological ethical, social and economic negative impact. Scientists need to concern these questions:
how to develop of a good (AI) society, how the role and responsibility of the government, the private sector, and the research community(including education),
in pursuing such a development, whether how the recommendation to support , such a (AI) system development may be in need of improvement.

However, none appears to deliver a comprehensive explicit vision of the role that (AI) system should play in mature information societies. Thus, (AI) 's potential
contribution to social good should include an in-depth plan for linking in a comprehensive socio-political design questions of responsibility of the different stakeholders,
of cooperation between them and of sharable values to understand of a good (AI) positive impact society, not a bad (AI) negative impact society.
Thus, the notion of mature information societies is introduced to bring the importance of addressing the current ethical challenges that (AI) poses in a comprehensive fashion.

It seems (AI) will invention will be human's moral societal consideration issue. It concerns our (AI) scientists' moral issue, how who invent (AI) system to apply
to which kind aspects. IF (AI) system was one direction on

war weapon tools to similar to soldier's personal mind or attacking behavior. Then, it will bring poor social
safety and poor economy growth our world, due to (AI) scientists' moral is low level.

Thus, the developed country US (AI) technological leader needs to focus on the impacts of (AI)-driven on the US job market and economy. It represents three
specific policy responses to the perceived impact of (AI) on the US economy. They include these three aspects such as: How to invest in and develop (AI) for its many benefits,
how to educate and train Americans for the jobs of the future and how to aid workers in the transition and empower workers to ensure broadly shared growth.

The future of (AI) influenced cyber conflicts need more than just the application of current and past solutions in order to ensure security and stability of societies, and avoid risks of escalation. To achieve this end, efforts to regulate cyber conflicts require an in-depth understanding of this new phenomenon, identify the changes brought about by cyber conflicts and the information and defines a set of shared values that will guide the stakeholders operating to avoid the international (AI) war occurrence. This becomes clear when considering for example, cyber deterrence. Deploying conventional (cold war) strategies to deter (AI)-influenced cyber conflicts
proves highly problematic and the urgent need to foster and coordinate new solutions able to account for the any kinds of conflicts of the cyber and of mature information
societies to avoid (AI) technological war occurrence in the future.

We hope that in the on-going international conversations and reviews, the US government with further specify how "

(AI) system invention law" fit into their vision of the future of society in this case the future of (AI) technological war and conflicts. Hence, (AI) scientists need to concern ethical issues related to (AI), like fairness, accountability and social justice can be addressed through increasing needs. Such as: how the creation of a new body focused on robotics and related (AI) system development to avoid to intent to apply weapon tools to provide advice on the policy, legl and consumer protection issues arising in these fields should be considered.

How to achieve ethical training of (AI) staff and ethical education of the public is certainly important responsibility for (AI) tools ethical behavior and design to the private sector and the citizens : of unique challenges that (AI) brings to society in terms in fairness, social equity and accountability are addresses. Thus, the development of the (AI) technology and defining good (AI) remains problematic. In particular, the US government's innovation driven approach to defining the potential, positive impact of (AI) shows that more could be done to ensure that the opportunities and advantages brought about by (AI) are shared by all society.

An initial on Robotics, based upon the ethical framework and guiding principles is proposed. It should be complementary to legislation and comprise ethical codes of conduct for Robotics researchers and designers, codes for research ethics committees as well as licenses (rights and duties) for designers and users. Thus, (AI) robotics invention of safety issues is very important consideration to any (AI) inventions or researchers. Every country's government

ought have legal guiding to control their robotics'
manufacturing intention.

If their robotics (AI) is applied to seem to be soldiers to
attack other countries to threaten their people's safety.
Then, those (AI) inventors or researchers need to be
punished by law.

In conclusion, I believe (AI) technology will be applied
to weapon, when it's technological development is nearly
mature to able to learn human's mind to do any behavior.
During (AI) technology reaches the mature stage, I predict
the (AI) weapon tool , e.g. (AI) soldiers will have chance to be
caused. This (AI) invention mature stage has these
characteristics such as:

When (AI) invention reaches this mature stage, computers
and robots will develop conscious, intelligent, personified
minds. Further, information technology devices and
(AI) systems will be implanted into humans, enhancing,
psychological and behavioral abilities and allowing for
direct communication with artificial intelligent minds.
There will be both artificial intelligence (AI) and
intelligence amplification (AI) in the relatively near future
stage.

During the (AI) invention reaches this mature stage,
these will be an ongoing multi-faceted integration of
information technologies and human life.
Humans and information technology will cooperate.
Humans will increasingly immerse their lives and minds in
(AI) systems of technological intelligence and
virtual reality. The distinction between humanity and
technology will increasingly close dependence.

During the (AI) invention mature stage reaches that the
environment will be infused with information technology,

becoming animated, communicative and
more intelligent. The aim between the artificial and the natural will increasing close dependence.

During the (AI) invention mature stage will expand through virtual reality, simulated and virtual reality will increasingly into normal reality, e.g. the
(AI) weapons is virtual reality to seem to be soldier weapon.

Finally, during the (AI) invention mature stage is as the global expression of the evolving human-technology integration a " world brain" and " world mind"
will emerge on the earth. This psychophysical (AI) weapon system will enhance and enrich the capacities of both individual and collective cognition. This (AI) weapon
system is a potential starting point toward the evolution of a cosmic brain and cosmic mind.

Thus, it is possible that the workshop raw data was a unique way in which (AI) could be weaponized to cause war, during the (AI) invention stage reaches the invention
mature stage. However, (AI) weapon manufacturing factory will be built possibly. In the future, how will we define and locate (AI) weapon factories. Especially, as these
factories are no longer solely buildings , but a mil of virtual and substantially different facilities, particularly as it shifts from a physical and development model to a distributed and flexible network. Needing minimal raw materials to develop (AI) weapons, the physical location of their (AI) factories could be anywhere and their identification from the outside, nearly impossible. Given the expanding uses for intelligent and super-intelligent (AI). How will we tell the different form a location that is manufacturing (AI) for the creation of weapons versus creating (AI) for an innovative new gaming platform?

In conclusion, human needs to consider every (AI) scientist's personal ethical or moral mind and research intention and (AI) system invention of (AI) weapon factories cause. During (AI) invention reaches the mature stage if human expects to avoid (AI) technological war occurrence in future one day. The technological development on autonomous military robots, ideally among relevant social groups and actors including human-rights, activists, researchers developers, engineers, philosophers, policy-makers, military authorities,
lawyers, journalists and the publish need to consider when human has effort to invent autonomous military robots successfully in the future one day. Finally, some ambitious countries or dominant global countries must like to apply (AI) autonomous military robots to be machine soldiers more than human soldiers if (AI) technology had reached the mature stage. So, future (AI) autonomous military robots will be the next choice of weapon to follow nuclear weapon. If civilians were used as a human (AI) soldiers, the weapon simply ignored them and targeted anyway. This scenario highlighted the dangers of proliferation and quick replication of autonomous weapons. Unlike nuclear weapon, a piece of code for (AI) artificial intelligent soldier could be obtained on the black market and replicated at little cost and the hardware for this type of weapon doesn't require costly or hard to obtain components and materials. Thus, (AI) artificial intelligent soldiers can be manufactured many at cheaper cost. Otherwise, manufacturing one nuclear bomb weapon will spend too much cost. Hence , it is possible that (AI) artificial intelligent soldier will be future new technological weapon to follow nuclear bomb weapon. Hence, any country government needs to legislate

to control any (AI) scientists' inventions whether they are attributed benefits or welfares to human or damage human's safety.

3
AI traveler behavior prediction

Q 29 Can artificial intelligent tools predict travelling consumer behavior in airline and air agent travelling market ?

I believe that applying (AI) big data tool to predict vehicle buyer consumption choice behavior, it is similar to predict traveler consumption choice behavior. In this chapter, I shall indicate how to apply (AI) big data gathering tool to predict vehicle buyer consumption choice behavior. Then, I shall its what its similar points to be applied to predict traveler consumption choice behavior.

Nowadays, many vehicle manufacturers hope their vehicles can attract to vehicle buyers to choose to buy their vehicles. However, there are many different brands of vehicles to provide to them to choose, so the vehicle market competition is very serious.

How to judge their different kinds of vehicle price which is reasonable acceptance to attract vehicle buyers to choose to buy the brand of vehicle manufacturers' any kinds of vehicles, e.g. fast speed sport style vehicles, comfortable and slow speed common cars, for four passengers common small size or more than four passengers common large car size?

How to evaluate the vehicle prices issue is important factor to influence vehicle buyers' choices. Either if the brand of vehicle price is too high to compare other brands of similar vehicle price, it will influence many vehicle buyers choose to buy other brands' vehicles or if the brand of vehicle price is too low, it will influence vehicle buyers feel this brand's vehicle machine quality or safe driving level or manufacturing steel material or speed or not comfortable sitting etc. different factors is worse to compare to other vehicle brands' similar vehicle products.

Thus, if the brand of vehicle manufacturers can predict how to design vehicles which can attract many vehicle buyers to choose to buy whose any vehicle products. What are future vehicle buyers' favorable vehicle styles? Then, the vehicle manufacturer can concentrate on manufacturing the kind style of vehicle products to sell already. It will reduce its vehicle manufacturing investment risk.

How to apply (AI) tools to predict vehicle buyers' behavioral consumption model? Whether artificial intelligent tools can predict automotive buyers' behavioral consumption model and predict future vehicle design trend. In fact, automotive brands and dealerships are facing an increasingly competition when attempting to manually gathering the vast quantities of data required to create customer focused programs that increase retention, ultimately new sales and service automotive business.

Building a based on that client's intrinsic needs and interests to any kinds of automotive vehicles at any given time. This is especially true in the automotive industry where the time span between purchases is measured in years. Because vehicle buyers would not like often to change their old vehicle to another new one. So, their decisions to buying another new vehicle, the time is usually after one year, even longer time. Hence, it seems any vehicles won't be frequent consumption products to the owned at least one vehicle family consumers (vehicle buyers). It implies that why vehicle manufacturers ought need to spend time to predict future vehicle buyer design choice for whole year vehicle buyer number growth because they won't often change preferable vehicle design to change another new vehicle more easily.

Hence, how to predict vehicle consumers' taste or preferable which styles of vehicle choices issues is very important. If the vehicle manufacturers can not manufacture any attractive vehicles to sell easily in this year. Then, it will lose time, money in this year because it won't know when the owned least one vehicle users or non-owned any vehicle users who will decide to buy one new vehicle or change another new vehicle ensure. The different brand vehicle dealers will possible wait more than one year to attract them to buy their vehicles if their styles are not attractive to compare other brands of vehicle competitors.

However, artificial intelligence and machine learning can help any vehicle manufacturers to find solution to solve patterns in highly to solve patterns in highly complex data-sets that are beyond the capability of a human brain, and then building and automatically acting on the customer insights it generates.

Given the automotive customer need for individualized communications, this technology is positioned to become a critical component of any successful vehicle retailer's domestic or/and overseas vehicle markets. How can vehicle manufacturers and retailers use (AI) to enhance their vehicle marketing campaigns? How will (AI) affect their vehicle sale marketing strategy? What criteria would they use when selecting on (AI) solution?

Vehicle consumers today are able to quickly access different brands of vehicle information, research vehicle products and reviews, negotiate prices and compare one vehicle brand or retailer to another resulting of the brands of vehicle customers. At the same time, the rise of " big -data mining", wearable devices that track user's every move and preference and greater contextualization in advertising and social media has resulted in consumer expectations of individualized. Thus, it seems that (AI) tools can be used to gather " big-data" and then they can make human's mind to analyze how to design kinds of vehicles to satisfy vehicle buyers' needs.

As automotive vehicle marketers can apply (AI) tools to achieve messaging strategies to meet the needs of this new generation of informed vehicle consumers, using data from a variety of sources to move from a variety of sources to move from mass- messaging to more personalized messages aimed at particular vehicle buyer segments, e.g. fast speed sport vehicle buyer segment, slow speed comfortable small size or large size of buyer segment. However, when 90% of vehicle marketers believe having a single vehicle buyer view is important, only 6% have achieved it.

However, one of the main issues vehicle marketers are facing the lack of capacity to efficiently sift through and analyze the massive vehicle buyer amounts of data required to create vehicle buyer individualized vehicle customer experiences easily. This is especially difficult for automotive dealers, the long periods between purchase cycles, and the highly considered nature of the vehicle purchase means that each vehicle dealer needs to not only track a large number of potential vehicle customers for an extremely long period of time, but each of those vehicle customers will generate a huge amount of different kinds of vehicle behavioral consumption data as they research their next vehicle purchase. However, by choosing the right (AI) technological tools and programs , vehicle dealers can solve this big data gathering challenge into a major advantage.

For Forrester vehicle brand example, vehicle consumers have more power over the Forrester vehicle brand's reputation than ever before. Mayne, L. (2014) indicated that Forrester calls this new (AI) tools is the " age of the vehicle customer", a 20 year business cycle in which the most successful vehicle enterprises will reinvent themselves to systematically understand and serve increasingly powerful vehicle consumers. To win in this new age, Forrester declares companies must become vehicle customer obsessed and the only sustainable competitive advantage is knowledge and engagement with customers, such as (AI) gathering data knowledge.

Thus, the biggest challenge vehicle businesses currently face is not the collection of a large quantity of vehicle consumer data, but what to do with that data once they have it. Even at a large vehicle data research firm, the data sets are often too big for a single analyze, or even a team of analysts to sort through and draw conclusion from. However, enter artificial intelligence and machine learning , an efficient technology solution that can continuously find patterns in highly complex data sets that are way beyond the capacity of a human brain and then automatic drive action based on the customer insights is generated.

What is (AI) machine learning tool? Machine learning is a type of (AI) that learns from data and is not explicitly program. Think Amazon, face book. Machine learning serves up relevant content based on an individual vehicle purchase behavior and experiences. More simply, machine learning is a computer program that can learn relationships between data, subject those learnings to errors functions, and then learn from its errors. The program in effect, trains itself.

Lee, T. (2016) explained that "Thus, (AI) tools can learn deep a more advanced branch of machine learning inspired by how our brain's nervous function, has also been found to be especial effective in identifying patterns from data."

When this way sound is complicated from a vehicle dealer perspective, the implementation of a marketing program driven by artificial intelligence can take care of these tasks in an automatic vehicle fashion with little to no manual intervention required from the staff at time vehicle stores.

In practice at a vehicle dealership, the program will continue track vehicle customer behavior online, merging that data with any offline source (like CRM or DMS data) and then analyze this aggregated vehicle buyer data set to predict what vehicle customer may be shopping for and what information they might like to relevance from different kinds style of vehicle design photos.

Q30 Why is (AI) big data gathering tool better than psychological and survey methods to predict traveler individual travel choice behavior?

Prediction travel behavioral consumption from psychology and survey methods.

How to predict travel consumption? It is one question to any travel agents concern to use what methods which can predict how many numbers of travelers where who will choose to go to travel more accurately. I think that who can consider how to predict travel behavioral consumption from psychology and survey travel choice prediction method, but it is better to apply (AI) big data gathering method to predict travel consumer's destination choice more accurate. The reason is as below:

The first reason is that traveler individual travel psychological desire is difficult to predict accurate more than (AI) big data gathering method, it is due that the data is past traveler's destination choice and travel package and ticket price actual data from (AI) big data gathering method. Otherwise, survey investigation is only traveler psychological thinking method. It lacks enough past actual traveler data gathering.

The second reason is that on the weakness of traveler individual psychological thinking view of survey investigation. It has evidence to support the relationship between self-identify threat and resistance to change travel behavior to any travelers, controlling for whose past travelling behavior, resistance to change if a psychological phenomenon of long standing interest in many applied branches of psychology.

Past travelling behavior has been acknowledged as a predictor of future action. Such as travelling behavior that is experienced as successful is likely to be repeated and may lead to habitual patterns. Some psychologists differentiate habit between two concepts, such as goal oriented and automatic oriented both. Although repeated past travelling behavior is addition goal oriented and automatic oriented. Further non-deliberative nature of habit may make appeals to judge and to predict future individual traveler's behavior accurately.

However, repeated one traveler will choose the destination to repeat to travel without a necessary constraint of goal orientation and automatic oriented both. So, it seems that psychological factor can influence any individual traveler why and how who choose to decide to repeat to choose the destination to travel.

So, survey investigation is only the traveler's thinking to answer the travel firm. It is not sure that the traveler's past travel experience is real answer. Otherwise, (AI) big data gathering method is computer gathering method which gather past traveler consumption actual data to analyze and conclude future traveler possible repeated travel destination choice and travel package choice more accurate.

The third reason is that on the strength of (AI) big data gathering method computer statistic view to predict future traveller consumer's destination and travel package choice. It is structural equation modeling is an extremely flexible linear-in-parameters multivariate statistical modeling technique. It has been used in modeling travel behavior and values since about 1980 year. It is a software method to handle a large number of variables, as well as unobserved variables specified as linear combinations (weighted averages) of the observed variable.

Q31 Can (AI) big data gather predict when climate or season will change to influence poor or better traveler behaviors?

(AI) big data tool can predict the flexibility of human travelling behavioral change is at least the result of one such mechanism, our ability to travel mentally in time and entertain potential future. Understanding of the impacts is holidays, particularly those involving travel.

Using focus groups research to explores tourists' awareness of the impacts of travel own climate change, examines the extent to which climate change features in holiday travel decisions and identifies some of the barriers to the adoption of less carbon intensive tourism practices.

The findings suggest many tourists don't consider climate change when planning their holidays. The failure of tourists to engage with the climate change to impact of holidays, combined with significant barriers to behavioral change, presents a considerable challenge in the tourism industry. In the future, computer (AI) big data tool can attempt to predict when the country's climate change to influence travelers to choose to go to the country to travel, e.g. next month or next half year or next year hot travelling destinations.

Tourism is a highly energy intensive industry and has only recently attracted attention as an important contributions to climate change through greenhouse gas emissions. It has been estimated that tourism contributes 5% of global carbon dioxide emissions. There have been a number of potential changes proposed for reducing the impact of air travel on climate change. These include technological changes, market based changes and behavioral changes.

However, the role that climate change plays in the holiday and travel decisions of global tourists. How the global tourists of the impacts travel has on climate change to establish the extent to which climate change, considerations features in holiday travel decision making processes and to investigate the major barriers to global tourists adopting less carbon intensive travel practices.

It will bring this question: Will tourists aware the impacts that their holidays and travel have on climate changes to influence their travelling decision?

When, it comes to understand individual traveler's behavioral change, wide range of conceptual theories have been developed, utilizing various social, psychological, subjective and objective variables in order to model travel consumption behavior. These theories of travel behavioral change operate at a number of different levels, including the individual level, the interpersonal level and community level. Whether pro-environmental behavior can be used to predict travel consumption behavior in a climate change. However, the question of what determines pro-environmental behavior in such a complex one that it can not be visualized through one single framework or diagram.

Despite the potentially high risk scenario for the tourism industry and the global environment, the tourism and climate change ought have close relationship.

However, (AI) big data tool can be applied to find what factors to influence the time of travelers' travelling choices. What are the important factors and variables which can limit tourism? e.g. money, time, family problem, extreme hot or cold weather change, air ticket price, journey attraction etc. variable factors.

Mention of holidays and travel were deliberately avoided in the recruitment process, so as not to create a connection factor to influence traveler's individual mind. However, the dismissal of alternative transportation modes can be conceived as either a structural barrier, in the sense that flying is perhaps the only realistic option to reach long-haul holiday destination, or a perceived behavioral control barriers in that an individual perceives flying as the only option open to whom.

The transportation tool factor will be depend to extent on the distance to the destination. This can also be interpreted in a social perspective as an intention with the resources available where much international tourism is structured around flying. To increase the availability of different transportation modes, tourists could choose holiday destination closer to home.

Finally, also how to predict future travel behavioral consumption. I feel that travel agents need to predict whether any country's random daily variation of weather factor is also important to influence travel behavior. e.g. in weather, temperature, rainfall and snowfall with traffic accidents factors will have relationship to cause travel demand.

Some scientists estimate suggest that when warmed temperatures and reduced snowfall are associated with a moderate decline in non-fatal accidents, they are also associated with a significant increase in fatal accidents. Thus increase in fatalities and temperature. Half of the estimated effect of temperature on fatalities is due to changes in the exposure to pedestrians, bicyclists and motorcyclists as temperature increase.

So, if any countries have rainfall, snowfall and low temperature to cause traffic accidents, whether this accident occurrence will influence the travelers who liking climb snow hills, riding bicycle, running sports who will avoid to travel to these countries' bad weather after occurs. So, why I feel that this natural climate factor will also be one serious factor to influence travel behavioral consumption. However, (AI) big data tool can predict more accurate than survey method when climate change to influence the country's climate to be poor, then it can predict when which countries are not popular acceptable to global country consumers' travel choice next month.

Q32 Is (AI) traveler behavioral prediction tool similar to manual psychological prediction method to be used to predict traveler behavior more accurate?

I shall explain how (AI) big data gathering technology can provide travelling businesses with better-informed decisions to drive top-line growth, deliver meaningful experience for travelling customers and smooth their path along the travelling consumer journey. The widely understood definition of (AI) involves the ability of machines or computers to learn human thinking, reasoning and decision-making abilities.

So, such as (AI) learning machine system can attempt to learn travelling consumer's travel destination or travel package thinking, judgement of their reasons why they choose to go to the destination to travel or why they choose to buy the travel package and learn how and why they make their past travelling decisions from their past travel big data gathering.

A Narrative science study in 2015 year identified that (AI) was being used primarily in voice recognition, machine learning virtual assistants and decision support. This study also highlighted the many branches of (AI) and that techniques and their definition are used interchangeably. It is possible that (AI) can be used to gather big data , then to analyze to help travel businesses to predict travelling consumer travel destination and travel package choice behaviors. For example, one of the most common techniques is traveler machine learning, where algorithms are used to perform tasks by learning from the airline or travel agent whose past all travelers' travelling destination choice and travel package choice historical data.

However, during 2017 year, search engines will begin to find what additional factors can influence past traveler personal travelling destination and travelling package travelling behavioral data into prediction of future travelling customer behavioral results, such as the online traveler (user's) history of travelling data searches, such as anywhere are the most popular travelling locations or travelling destinations and previously captures conservations.

Artificial intelligence will use this past travelling destinations and travelling package information to power predictive search results, e.g. predictive future travelling consumer's choice behavioral processing for where will be their preferable travelling destination choice and how to design travelling package to satisfy future travelling clients' needs.

Predictive search will improve the quality of online travelling search results, and provide new insights into travelling consumers' travelling destination and package behavior and the moments which matter to them. Search will give recommendation into tailored how travelling consumer individual travelling destination choice in travelling decision making process. Several of the largest online platforms already use (AI) travelling machine learning to improve predictive travelling consumer behavioral search results.

For example, Google's rank brain technology adds research by understanding the context in which the travelling consumer has entered it. Over time, rank brain will learn further from user behaviors Amazon's DSSTNE (pronouned destiny) learns from shoppers' purchasing habits and consumption behavior to offer better product recommend actions, which Amazon can offer before a consumer has entered anything into the search bar.

Such as (AI) big data can gather past online travelers' e-ticket purchase transactions to conclude that online traveler's travelling choice habits and online traveler consumption behavior to offer better travelling destinations and travelling package opinions to travel agents or airlines. However, this technology is not independent of human input. For example, Google engineers will periodically retain the rank brain system to improve the models it uses.

For another example, in 2016 year , Apple computer revamped its travelling scene photos app to allow travelling consumers to search for specific travelling destinations in the travelling scene phots, they want to find anywhere travelling destination photos, not just dates and locations. Each travelling photo that an intelligent phone or intelligent pad user takes goes through 11 billion computations, so that travelling scene photos can understand exactly where is the travelling destination photography to let online travelling consumer to feel anywhere they plan to go to the location to travel. So, (AI) learning machine can make online travelling photos more attractive to influence potential travelers choose to the destination to travel after they see the travelling destination scene photos from internet.

It seems that in future, (AI) machine learning will allow online travelling search to evolve even further. Search engineers will deliver refined recommendations to airlines' online traveler e-ticket search users and use less human input to predict travelling consumers' needs from internet channel. For IBM computer example, it indicated 90% of the data that exists today has been created in the last two years.

This huge explosion of past traveler's e-ticket consumption

data gives the opportunity to quickly spot and react to the latest trends, fashion and fads among its travelling clients and potential clients. This will allow airline or travel agent companies to better engage with younger travelling consumers, who gain influence access to the latest travelling destination and package trends.

They associate with to help define who they are as individuals. Thus, travelling company brands have to identify and make use of them before travelling consumers move on, but the vast quantity of past e-ticket purchase data available makes from internet channel. This a resource-intensive task. For next example, Lesara, a based online clothes store, uses this machine learning to inform its product decision often gathering information from internal and external sources.

When its trends -spotting shoes. Lesara has a range of over 20 styles and sells hundreds of pairs a day. It focus on giving consumers, the very latest trends allow Lesara to develop on average of 50,000 new items each year. It compared to 11,000 old items each year. Thus, travelling agents or airlines can attempt to apply (AI) big data gathering method to gather all past e-ticket purchase data, concerns where they prefer to choose to go to the destinations to travel and what travelling packages are the most attractive to the travelers to choose to buy. It aims to help them to predict where future travelers will prefer to choose to go to travel or what travelling package they will prefer to choose to buy next year.

For another (AI) big data prediction example, Lesara is one online clothes store, uses machine learning decisions after gathering information from internal and external sources. One of its most popular products, shoes with LED started life when its trend spotting software flagged up a blogger wearing similar shoes. Now Lesara has a range of over 20 styles and sells hundreds of pairs a day. Its focus on giving consumers the very latest trends allows Lesara to develop an average of 50,000 new items each year, compared to 11,000 for its competitor Lara.

It seems (AI) big data gathering machine learning can help Lesara business to predict what kinds of shoes design or style that shoe consumers will prefer choose to buy in future shoe market trend. Thus, Lesara can predict shoe consumers' taste successfully and it can manufacture many attractive style of shoes.

(AI) machine learning can gather global past shoe consumer's shoe shopping experiences, then analyzes to make conclusion to give lesara recommendation successfully. This will make the experience more enjoyable for shoe consumers and allow Lesara to advert whose different new style or design of shoes to deliver them move relevant messages by understanding the context of the experience.

So, online travel agents or online airline can also attempt to apply (AI) big data gathering method to predict where travelers will prefer to go to travel and how they ought design travelling packages to attract them to choose to buy next year. Hence, (AI) big data gathering technology can conclude how to design traveler agents' travelling package products to be the most attractive to excite many travelers choose to buy their travelling package, due to it has more accurate to predict travelling consumer destination and travelling package choice behaviors to compare human themselves prediction judgement effort, e.g. travelling survey or marketing research, or telephone enquire. It seems that (AI) machine judgement effort is more accurate to compare to human judgment effort in travelling industry.

What are the difference between (AI) and manual psychological method to predict Future travel consumption behavior ?

Can (AI) big data gathering tool predict traveler individual habitual behavior , e.g. renting travel transportation tools ?

Can (AI) big data gathering tool can predict past traveler destination and travelling package choice habit and it can be intended to predict of future traveler behavior to people are creatures of habits judgement of future anywhere travelling destination choice next year or next month or next half year destination prediction ?

Many of human's everyday goal-directed behaviors are performed in a habitual fashion, the transportation made and route one takes to work, one's choice of breakfast. Habits are formed when using the some behavior frequently and a similar consistency in a similar context for the some purpose whether the individual past travel consumption model will be caused a habit to whom. e.g. choosing whom travel agent to buy air ticket or traveling package; choosing the same or similar countries' destinations to go to travel ; choosing the business class or normal (general) class of quality airlines to catch planes.

Does habitual rent traveling car tools use not lead to more resistance to change of travel mode? It has been argued that past behavior is the best predictor of future behavior to travel consumption. If individual traveler's past consumption behavior was always reasoned, then frequency of prior travel consumption behavior should only have an indirect link to the individual traveler's behavior. It seems that renting travel car tools to use is a habit example. So, a strong rent traveling car tools useful habit makes traveling mode choice. People with a strong renting of traveling car tools of habit should have low motivation to attend to gather any information about public transportation in their choice of travelling country for individual or family or friends members during their traveling journeys.

Even when persuasive communication changes the traveler whose attitudes and intention, in the case of individual traveler or family travelers with a strong renting travel car tools habit. It is difficult to change whose travel behaviors to choose to catch public transportation in whose any trips in any countries. However, understanding of travel behavior and the reasons for choosing one mode of transportation over another. The arguments for rent traveling car tools to use, including convenience, speed, comfort and individual freedom and well known.

Increasingly, psychological factors include such as, perceptions, identity, social norms and habit are being used to understand travel mode choice. Whether how many travel consumers will choose to rent traveling car tools during their trips in any countries. It is difficult to estimate the numbers. As the average level of renting travel car tools of dependence or attitudes to certain travel package policies from travel agents. Instead different people must be treated in different ways because who are motivated in different ways and who are motivated by different travel package policies ways from travel agents.

In conclusion, the factors influence whose traveler's individual traveler destination choice behavior The factors include either who chooses to rent traveling car tools or who chooses to catch public transportation when who individual goes to travel in alone trip or family trip. It include influence mode choice factors, such as social psychology factor and marketing on segmentation factor both to influence whose transportation choice of behavior in whose trip. So, (AI) big data can be attempted to gather past traveler transportation tool choice, rent travelling car tools choice or catching public transportation tools choice to predict where destination can provide what kind of transportation tool to attract many travelers to choose to go to the place to travel.

How (AI) big data determine future travel behavior from past travel experience and perceptions of risk and safety for the benefits to travel consumers?

How (AI) big data determine future travel behavior from past travel experience and perceptions of risk and safety for the benefits to travel consumers? Why does individual traveler avoid certain destination(s) is(are) as relevant to tourist decision making as why who chooses to travel to others?

Perceptions of risk and safety and travel experience are likely to influence travel decisions. If travel agents had efforts to predict future travel behavior to guess whether travelers will feel where is(are) risk and unsafe to cause who does not choose to go to the country to travel. Then, the travel agents will avoid to choose to spend much time to design the different traveling package to attract their potential travel consumers to choose to travel. The reason is because in the case of individual traveler's tourism experience, the traveler whose past disappointment travel experience (psychological risk) will be a serious threat to the traveler's health or life (health, physical or terrorism risk). The past safety or unhealthy risk to the country(countries) will influence the traveler decides to choose not to go to the countries(country) to travel again in the future.

Q 33 How (AI) bring push and pull motivation to influence any traveler who chooses where is whose preferable travelling destination ?

How to apply (AI) big data to predict individual traveler's behavioral intention of choosing a travel destination?
Understanding why people travel and what factors influence their behavioral intention of choosing a travel destination is beneficial to tourism planning and marketing. In general, an individual's choice of a travel destination into two forces.
The first force is the push factor that pushes an individual away from home and attempt to develop a general desire to go somewhere, without specifying where that may be.
The other force is the pull factor that pull an individual toward in destination, due to a region-specific or perceived attractiveness of a destination. The respective push and pull factors illustrate that people travel because who are pushed by whose internal motives and pulled by external forced of a destination. However, the decision making process leading to the choice of a travel destination is a very complex process.
For example, a Taiwanese traveler who might either choose new travel destination of Hong Kong or another old travel Asia destinations again or who also might choose any one of Western country, as a new travel destination. The travel agents can predict where who will have intention to choose to travel from whose past behavior and attitude, subjective and perceived behavioral control model. When (AI) big data gather past every country traveler number who chose to go to which countries to travel in order to judge where destinations will be the country travelers' travelling choice destinations in the future.

The factors influence where is the traveler choice, include personal safety, scenic beauty, cultural interest, climate changing, transportation tools, friendliness of local people, price of trip, trip package service in hotels and restaurants, quality and variety of food and shopping facilities and services etc. needs. So, whose factors will influence where is the individual travel's choice. It seems every traveler whose choice of travel process, will include past behavior. e.g. travelling experience, travelling habit, then to choose the best seasoned travelling action to satisfy whose travel needs. This process is the individual traveler's psychological choice process, who must need time to gather information to compare concerning of different travel packages, destination scene, climate change, transportation tools available to the destination, air ticket price etc. these factors, then to judge where is the best right destination to travel in the right time.

Hence, (AI) big data can gather past different countries' climate changing data, transportation tool changing data, destination scene environment changing etc. different data to give opinions to travelling businesses whether any country's these above factors will influence about how many traveler number will be increase or decrease in the future.

Why and how (AI) can expect to predict what motivation and attitude factors are to traveler behavior?

Social psychology is concerned with gaining insight into the psychological of socially relevant behaviors and the processes. For instance, on a global level bad influence to global warming, it influences some countries extreme cold or hot bad climate changing occurrence, then it ought influence some travelers' behavioral decision to change their mind to choose some countries to go to travel at the moment which do not occur extreme hot or cold climate (temperature). e.g. above than 40 degree in summer or below than 0 degree in winter. Due to the extreme climate changing environment in the countries, it will cause them to feel uncomfortable to play during their trips. So, the global warming causes to climate changing factor will influence the numbers of travel consumption to be reduced possibly. This is global climate changing environment factor influences to bad or uncomfortable social psychological feeling to global travelers' mind of traveling decision. What is individual traveler expectation, motivation and attitude? Tourism sector includes inbound (domestic) tourism and outbound (overseas) tourism both incomes to any countries. According to recent article, a tourist behavior model has been developed, called the expectation, motivation and attitude (EMA) model (Hsu et al., 2010).

This model focuses on the pre-visit stage of tourists by modeling the behavioral process by incorporating expectation, motivation and attitude. Travel motivation is considered as an essential component of the behavioral process, which has been increasing attention from the travel; industry. The economic approach defines "tourism" is an identifiable nationally important industry. It includes the component activities of transportation, accommodation, recreation, food and related service. So, tourism behavioral consumption is concerned the individual tourist's usual habituate of the industry which responds to whose needs, and of the impacts that both the tourist and the tourism industry have on the socio-cultural, economic and physical environment.

However, travel motivation means how to understand and predict factors that influence travel decision making.

According to Backman and others (1995, p.15), motivation is conceptually viewed as " a state of need, a condition that services as a driving force to display different kind of behavior toward certain types of activities, developing preferences, arriving at some expected satisfactory outcome." So, motivation and expectancy which has close relationship to any tourist before who decided to do any tourism of behavior.

Some economists confirmed motivation and expectancy which has relations, such as expectation of visiting an outbound destination has a direct effect on motivation to visit the destination; motivation has a direct effect on attitude toward visiting the destination; expectation of visiting the outbound destination has a direct affection on attitude toward visiting the destination and motivation has a mediating effect on the relationship in between expectation and attitude.

Hence, (AI) big data can gather all the country's climate environment change, transportation tool change, entertainment scene change, hotel price and restaurant price change etc. data to give opinions whether the country will attract how many traveler to choose to go to travel in the year.

Q34 What is (AI) deep learning techniques to forecast travelling environment behavioral consumption?

Prediction how many travelers will choose to go to the country to travel. It is similar to apply deep-learning technology to predict how to raise the agricultural farming productivity in the agricultural export country.

The (AI) deep-learning technology leads to performance enhancement and generalization of artificial intelligent technology. It influences the global leader in the field of information technology has declared its intention to utilize the deep-learning technology to solve environmental problems, such as climate change.

So, it will help agriculture farming businesses can raise any plant food: vegetable, fruit, rice which grow up very easily if farmers can apply (AI) deep-learning technology to solve environment problems to influence their plant food grow. If the whole year seasonal change is very good and it is suitable for any plant food to grow in farming land easily, e.g. rain is enough and soil is enough for any plant food to grow in the farm lands. Then, fruit, rice, vegetable etc. agriculture businesses will have much beneficial attribution to global farmers.

The question is how to use deep-learning technologies in the environmental field to predict the status of pro-environmental consumption. We predicted the pro-environmental consumption index based on Google search query data, using a recurrent neural network (RNN model). To certify the accuracy of the index, we compared the prediction accuracy of the RNN model with that of the ordinary least square and artificial necessary network models.

For example, the RNN model predicts the pro-environmental consumption index better than any other model. we expect the RNN model to perform still better in a big data environment because the deep-learning technologies would be increasingly as the volume of data grows. So, deep-learning technologies could be useful in environmental forecasting to prevent damage caused by climate change to influence any rice, vegetable, tomato, potato, fruit etc. different plant food grow in any countries' farming land easily.

For South Korea example, over 800 government agencies spent 2.2 trillion Korea won on eco-products in 2014 year. However, green products are rarely purchased outside these agencies. This phenomenon occurs because there is a gap between consumer attitudes and behavior , that is environmental attitude is a major factor in decision making vis-a-vis the consumption of " green" food and services (Jorea Ministry of Environment, 2015).

Therefore, it is necessary to understand those consumer attitude, that will lead to sustainability-conductive behavior and consumption. (AI) Deep learning system can be applied to attempt understand those traveler attitude to environment protection to fly to which country. For example, (AI) deep learning system can attempt to gather data concerns how many Hong Kong people concern air pollution challenge to influence their health, then it can attempt to predict how many Hong Kong travelers do not choose to go China travel, due to the air pollution challenge to influence their health.

The (AI) deep learning techniques to forecast travelling environment behavioral consumption may include as below:

Environmental travel consumption prediction

Recently, many researchers have studied pro-environmental consumption and household indexes as well as suicide rate predictions using messages posted by internet users on Google trend, Tweets etc. channel.

Whether can environmental consumption be predicted by (AI) deep-learning technological internet channel to influence how many travelers choose to go to the country to travel?

How can impact the pro-environmental consumption attitudes of green policies to influence how many travelers choose to go to the country to travel?

For example, Korea scientists estimated pro-environmental attitudes using search query data provided by Google trend and confirmed through regression analysis, that pro-environmental attitude has a positive correlation with the pro-environmental attitude index. They also explained that environment-friendly attitude of residents plan an important role in policy making. In the past, most household consumption indexed were calculated through surveys, but (AI) deep-learning technological tool " big data" have recently gained research attention (Lee et al. 2016). So, (AI) deep learning technology can attempt to gather whether how many Korea residents who concern environment pollution to influence their eating green food attitude then to judge whether how many Korea residents hope to leave their country to travel anywhere either high risk environment pollution countries to travel or low risk environment pollution countries to travel in the future.

It seems that (AI) deep-learning technology can help agricultural export countries' farmers , e.g. US, UK, Canada, New Zealand, Australia, Japan, China, India etc. they can predict environmental behavioral consumption to any rice, tomato, potato , fruit, vegetable etc. plant food consumers. The beneficial advantages to them include as below:

(a) Assuming they know their countries' weather, when it has less rain to cause drought or when it has more rain in any seasonal time in the year. They can choose not to grow any kinds of above these plant food to avoid loss.

(b) They can make any kinds of above these plant food price raising after their prediction of these bad seasonal time to cause their plant food shortage supply challenge. Because these plant food consumers' demand number is more, but the supply of these above plant food supply number is less. However, due to they had predicted when the bad seasonal time can not allow them to grow these above plant food before. So, they have enough time to grow many these above plant food number in predictive good seasonal time to prepare to supply to their plant food import countries' plant food consumers to eat. Thus, these predictive environmental consumption plant food export countries can raise their plant food price to sell to them. When, the other non-pre-predictive environmental consumption plant food export countries can not supply any one of those plant food to them to eat, due to the bad climate to cause them can't grow any one of these plant food to export to sell.

Thus, (AI) deep-learning technology can be applied to predict how to raise the plant food supply number in order to raise price to the import plant food countries consumers to eat, due to they feel difficult to buy these plant food to eat in the bad climate seasonal time in whole year.

(c) (AI) deep-learning technology can help climate scientists to find what reasons cause their countries; rain sudden increases or cause their countries' rain sudden decreases. After its gathering data analysis, it can assist climate scientists to find solution methods to attempt to control the rain level can be right falling down level to let agricultural export farmers who can grow their plant food to sell to agricultural import countries in whole year.

(d) The agricultural export countries' farmers can apply (AI) deep-learning technology to help them to choose whether growing which kinds of plant food in that whether climate time to earn more plant food consumption number more easily.

Due to the agricultural countries climate will often change, for example, tomato, potato, rice, fruit etc. plant food can be adapt to grow in more rain time, but vegetable can not be adapt to grow in more rain time. If farmers can apply this technology to predict when it will have move rain or when it will have less rain to fall down in their countries. Then, they can choose to grow which kinds of plant food number more, in the suitable seasonal climate time in order to raise plant food growing number productivities to supply to sell to satisfy any agricultural food import countries' demand effectively.

(e) (AI) deep-learning technology can help agricultural import countries to solve agricultural food shortage challenge in long term. When this technology can be popular to base applied by the agricultural plant food export countries. It will solve global agricultural food shortage challenge. For example, when one agricultural export countries' farmers can popular accept to apply this technology to predict when to grow which kinds of plant food more to rise number productivities to sell. e.g. vegetable, fruit, rice Besides another agricultural export countries' farmers can also accept to apply this technology to predict when to grow plant food, e.g. potato, tomato to raise number productivities to sell. Then, they can concentrate on growing the specific kinds of plant food in order to raise the specific plant food number productivities in every seasonal change time every month. Then, global agricultural plant food supply must be raised, due to these predictive environmental change farmers can know who ought grow which kinds of plant food to sell to raise number productivities.

Consequently, (AI) deep learning can gather where countries will have high risk environment pollution to influence health food supply. Then, it can give opinions to travelling businesses when these high risk environment pollution countries will encounter the traveler number to be decreased, due to the environment pollution serious challenge will occur.

How to use qualitative of travel behavioral method to predict future travel consumption from (AI) big data ?

I also suggest to use qualitative of travel behavioral method to predict future travel consumption. Methods such as focus groups interviews and participant observer techniques can be used with quantitative approaches on their own to fill the gaps left by quantitative techniques. These insights have contributed to the development of increasingly sophisticated models to forecast travel behavior and predict changes in behavior in response to change in the transportation system. I shall indicate the weaknesses of human travelling investigation methods as below:

First, survey methods restrict not only the question frame but the answer frame as well, anticipating the important issues and questions and the responses. However, these surveys methods are not well suited to exploratory areas of research where issues remain unidentified and the researched seek to answer the question "why?".

Second, data collection methods using traditional travel diaries or telephone recruitment can under represent certain segments of the population, particularly the older persons with little education, minorities and the poor. Before the survey, focus group for example can be used to identify what socio-demographic variables to include in the survey, how best to structure the diary, even what incentives will be most effective in increasing the response rate.

After the survey, focus, focus groups can be used to build

explanations for the survey results to identify the "why" of the results as well as the implications. One Asia Pacific survey research result was made by tourism market investigation before. It indicated the travel in Asia Pacific market in the past, had often been undertaken in large groups through leisure package sold in bulk, or in large organized business groups, future travelers will be in smaller groups or alone, and for a much wider range of reasons.

Significant new traveler segments, such as female business traveler. The small business traveler and the senior traveler, all of which have different aspirations and requirements from the travel experience.

Moreover, Asia tourism market will start to exist behaviors in the adoption of newer technologies, a giving the traveler new ways to manage the travel experience, creating new behaviors. This with provide new opportunities for travel providers. The use of mobile devices, smartphones, tablets etc. and social media are the obvious findings to become an integral part of the travel experience. Thus, quality method can attempt to predict Asia Pacific tourism market development in the future. It is such as (AI) big data gathering tool can give traveler quality opinions to any travelling businesses to make the more accurate where will be the popular travel destination choice next month or next half year or next year.

However, improving the predictive power of travel behavior models and to increase understanding travel behavior which lies in the use of panel data(repeated measures from the same individuals). Whereas, cross-sectional data only reveal inter-individual differences at one moment in time, panel data can reveal intra-individual changes over time. In effect, panel data are generally better suited to understand and predict (changes in) travel behavior. However, a substantial proportion was also observed to transition between very different activity/ travel patterns over time, indicating that from one year to the next, many people renegotiated their activity/travel patterns.

How to apply advanced traveler information systems (ATIS) to predict future travelling behavior?

Nowadays, information can impact on traveler behavior and network performance. For example, when steadily growing levels of vehicle ownership and vehicle miles traveled information has been identified as a potential strategy towards man aging travel demand, optimizing transportation networks and better utilizing available capacity. Toward, this goal to predict further tourist behavioral consumption. Many countries, government tourism development institutes has applied advanced traveler information systems (ATIS) which travel behavior models and high-fidelity network performance models made increasingly feasible through the rapid advances in computer power. Crucial components of this problem domain are the modeling of individual tourist drivers' response to travel information and the development accurate guidance of relevance to real would trip makers. So, this advanced traveler information systems (ATIS) can assist the tourist who like to rent travelling car tools to travel in any countries own free traveler information systems service conveniently. Also, this travel information system can be intended to assist travelers to make better travel choices. e.g. this system can improve the decision making of individual traveler rather than improvements of network performance overall. So, we need to understand how tourists make their travel plans. Also, understanding decision process that lead to booking of the trip is equally important, as it allows of a potential behavior.

How can online tourism sale channel influence traveling consumption of behavior?

Nowadays, internet is popular, it seems that booking air ticket behavior of using internet is predicted to influence overall tourism air tickets payment method. Tourism industry has grown in the previous several decades. Despite its global impact, questions related to better understanding of tourists and whose habits. Using online travel air ticket booking benefits include booking electronic air tickets can be made from entering any electronic travel agents websites in the short time and electronic travel ticket payers do not need leave home, who can pay visa card to pre booking any electronic travel ticket from online channel conveniently.

How can analyze activity based travel demand ?

Nowadays, human are concerning the traffic congestion and air quality deterioration, the supply oriented focus of transportation planning has expanded to include how to manage travel demand within the available transportation supply. Consequently, there has been an increasing interest in travel demand management strategies, such as congestion pricing that attempts to change aggregate travel demand. The prediction aggregate level, long term travel demand to understanding disaggregate level (i.e. individual levels) behavioral responses to short term demand policies, such as ride sharing incentives, congestion pricing and employer based demand management schemes, alternate work schedules, telecommuting limitation of travel agent traditionally work nature shall influence oriented trip based travel modelling passenger travel demand indirectly.

Finally, online travel purchase will be popular to influence the number of travel behavioral consumption nowadays. Any travel package products can be sold from websites to attract travelers to choose to pre-book air ticket for any trips conveniently. In the past ten years, the internet has become the predominant carrier of all types of information and transactions. Regarding travel decisions, internet has also become an important sales channels for the travel industry, because it is associated with comparably lower distribution and sales costs, but also because it adapts to high supply and demand dynamics in this industry. Consequently, the travel and tourism industry tries to increase the internet sale specific share of sales volumes. So, internet sale channel has changed travel consumption behavioral pattern and characteristics and travel experience. For example, Switzerland has one of the highest population-to-computer ratio in Europe. It is also one of the most highly internet penetrated countries in terms of use of the WWW on a day-to-day basis, with more than 75 percent of the population older than 14 years using the WWW daily (ICT, 2005).

The reason of booking online tourism may include: convenience, fast transaction, finding traveling package choice easily, more airline seats available. So, online booking tourism will influence the traditional tourism agents visiting of sales and air tickets and travelling package numbers to be decreased. Finally, the online booking tourism market shares will be expanded to more than traditional tourism agents visits sale market in the future one day. So, the travel agents who still use the traditional tourism visiting sale channel which ought raise whose features to compare to differ to online tourism sale channel if these traditional tourism agents want to keep competitive ability in tourism industry for long term.

What is (AI) actively based patterns of urban population of travel behavioral prediction method?

Actively based patterns of urban population. It is a method of motivational framework means in which societal constraints and inherent individual motivations interact to shape activity participation patterns. It can be used to predict one city or urban the numbers of travel demand in the year. It has two elements: First, capability constraints refer to constraints are imposed by biological needs, such as eating and sleeping and/or resources, such as income, availability of cars etc. to undertake the urban or city's family activities in the year. Second, coupling constraints define where, when and the duration of planning activities that are to be pursued with other individuals. So, this method needs to gather information (data) to get the relationship between activities, travel and spending work time and space time to evaluate whether there are how many families who have real needs to spend time to go to travel in the year.

What is (AI) trip based versus activity based approaches?

What is trip based versus activity based approaches? The fundamental difference between the trip-based and activity based approaches is that the former approach directly focuses on trips without explicit recognition of the motivation or reason for the trips and travel. The activity based approach , on the other hand, views travel as a demand derived from the need to pursue travel activities.

So, it is better understand the individual or family behavior basis for individual or family travelling decision regarding participation in travelling activities in certain places or cities or countries at given times and hence the resulting travel needs. This behavioral basis includes all the factors that influence the why, how, when and where of performed activities and resulting individuals and household, the cultural/social norms of the community and the travel surrounding environment.

Another difference between the two approaches is in the way travel is represented. The trip based approach represents travel as a collection of trips. Each trip is considered as independent of other trips, without considering the inter-relationship in the choice attributes , such as time, destination and mode of different trips. As tours are chains of trips beginning and ending at a same location , say home or work. The tour based representation helps maintain the consistency across and capture the interdependency and consistency of the modeled choice attributed among the trips of the same tour.

In addition to the tour based representation of travel, the activity based approach focuses on sequences or patterns of activity participation and travel behavior, using the whole day or longer periods of time is the unit of analysis. Such as approach can address travel demand management issues through an examination of how people modify their activity participation, for example, will individuals substitute more out-of-home activities for in home activities in the evening of who arrived early form work due-to a work schedule change?

The major difference between trip based and the activity based approaches is in the way, the time dimension of activities and travel is considered. In the trip based approach, time is reduced to being simply a cost making a trip and a day's viewed as a combination, defined peak and off peak time periods. On the other hand, activity based approach views individuals' activity travel patterns are a result of their time use decisions with a continuous time domain. As individuals have 24 hours in a day or multiples of 24 hours for longer periods of time and decide how to use that travel among or allocate that time to activities and travel and with who, subject to their socio-demographic, transportation system and other and scheduling of trips. So, determining the impact of travel demand management policies on time use behavior is an important step to assessing the impact of such policies on individual travel behavior. The final major difference between this two approaches relates to the level of aggregation. In the trip based approach, most aspect of travel, e.g. number of trips etc. are analyzed at an aggregate level.

Consequently, trip based methods accommodate the effect of socio-demographic attributes of households and individuals in a very limited fashion, which limits the activity of the method to evaluate travel impacts of long term socio-demographic characteristics of the individuals who actually make the activity travel choices and the travel service characteristics of the surrounding environment. So, the activity based models are better equipped to forecast the longer term changes in travel demand in response composition and the travel environment of urban areas. Also, using activity based models, the impact of policies can be assessed by predicting individual level behavioral responses instead of employing trip based statistical averages that are aggregated over defined demographic segments.

What methods can predict future travel behavioral consumption ?

How to use qualitative of travel behavioral method to predict future travel consumption from (AI) big data ?

I also suggest to use qualitative of travel behavioral method to predict future travel consumption. Methods such as focus groups interviews and participant observer techniques can be used with quantitative approaches on their own to fill the gaps left by quantitative techniques. These insights have contributed to the development of increasingly sophisticated models to forecast travel behavior and predict changes in behavior in response to change in the transportation system. I shall indicate the weaknesses of human travelling investigation methods as below:

First, survey methods restrict not only the question frame but the answer frame as well, anticipating the important issues and questions and the responses. However, these surveys methods are not well suited to exploratory areas of research where issues remain unidentified and the researched seek to answer the question "why?".

Second, data collection methods using traditional travel diaries or telephone recruitment can under represent certain segments of the population, particularly the older persons with little education, minorities and the poor. Before the survey, focus group for example can be used to identify what socio-demographic variables to include in the survey, how best to structure the diary, even what incentives will be most effective in increasing the response rate.

After the survey, focus, focus groups can be used to build explanations for the survey results to identify the "why" of the results as well as the implications. One Asia Pacific survey research result was made by tourism market investigation before. It indicated the travel in Asia Pacific market in the past, had often been undertaken in large groups through leisure package sold in bulk, or in large organized business groups, future travelers will be in smaller groups or alone, and for a much wider range of reasons.

Significant new traveler segments, such as female business traveler. The small business traveler and the senior traveler, all of which have different aspirations and requirements from the travel experience.

Moreover, Asia tourism market will start to exist behaviors in the adoption of newer technologies, a giving the traveler new ways to manage the travel experience, creating new behaviors. This with provide new opportunities for travel providers. The use of mobile devices, smartphones, tablets etc. and social media are the obvious findings to become an integral part of the travel experience. Thus, quality method can attempt to predict Asia Pacific tourism market development in the future. It is such as (AI) big data gathering tool can give traveler quality opinions to any travelling businesses to make the more accurate where will be the popular travel destination choice next month or next half year or next year.

However, improving the predictive power of travel behavior models and to increase understanding travel behavior which lies in the use of panel data(repeated measures from the same individuals). Whereas, cross-sectional data only reveal inter-individual differences at one moment in time, panel data can reveal intra-individual changes over time. In effect, panel data are generally better suited to understand and predict (changes in) travel behavior. However, a substantial proportion was also observed to transition between very different activity/ travel patterns over time, indicating that from one year to the next, many people renegotiated their activity/travel patterns.

3.3 How to apply advanced traveler information systems (ATIS) to predict future travelling behavior?

Nowadays, information can impact on traveler behavior and network performance. For example, when steadily growing levels of vehicle ownership and vehicle miles traveled information has been identified as a potential strategy towards man aging travel demand, optimizing transportation networks and better utilizing available capacity. Toward, this goal to predict further tourist behavioral consumption. Many countries, government tourism development institutes has applied advanced traveler information systems (ATIS) which travel behavior models and high-fidelity network performance models made increasingly feasible through the rapid advances in computer power. Crucial components of this problem domain are the modeling of individual tourist drivers' response to travel information and the development accurate guidance of relevance to real would trip makers. So, this advanced traveler information systems (ATIS) can assist the tourist who like to rent travelling car tools to travel in any countries own free traveler information systems service conveniently. Also, this travel information system can be intended to assist travelers to make better travel choices. e.g. this system can improve the decision making of individual traveler rather than improvements of network performance overall. So, we need to understand how tourists make their travel plans. Also, understanding decision process that lead to booking of the trip is equally important, as it allows of a potential behavior.

How can online tourism sale channel influence traveling consumption of behavior?

Nowadays, internet is popular, it seems that booking air ticket behavior of using internet is predicted to influence overall tourism air tickets payment method. Tourism industry has grown in the previous several decades. Despite its global impact, questions related to better understanding of tourists and whose habits. Using online travel air ticket booking benefits include booking electronic air tickets can be made from entering any electronic travel agents websites in the short time and electronic travel ticket payers do not need leave home, who can pay visa card to pre booking any electronic travel ticket from online channel conveniently.

popular to influence the number of travel behavioral consumption nowadays. Any travel package products can be sold from websites to attract travelers to choose to pre-book air ticket for any trips conveniently. In the past ten years, the internet has become the predominant carrier of all types of information and transactions. Regarding travel decisions, internet has also become an important sales channels for the travel industry, because it is associated with comparably lower distribution and sales costs, but also because it adapts to high supply and demand dynamics in this industry. Consequently, the travel and tourism industry tries to increase the internet sale specific share of sales volumes. So, internet sale channel has changed travel consumption behavioral pattern and characteristics and travel experience. For example, Switzerland has one of the highest population-to-computer ratio in Europe. It is also one of the most highly internet penetrated countries in terms of use of the WWW on a day-to-day basis, with more than 75 percent of the population older than 14 years using the WWW daily (ICT, 2005).

The reason of booking online tourism may include: convenience, fast transaction, finding traveling package choice easily, more airline seats available. So, online booking tourism will influence the traditional tourism agents visiting of sales and air tickets and travelling package numbers to be decreased. Finally, the online booking tourism market shares will be expanded to more than traditional tourism agents visits sale market in the future one day. So, the travel agents who still use the traditional tourism visiting sale channel which ought raise whose features to compare to differ to online tourism sale channel if these traditional tourism agents want to keep competitive ability in tourism industry for long term.

35 Can apply (AI) big data gathering method predict senior age will be main travelling target?

In the past, Germany government had established tourism survey analysis to analyze survey data in order to arrive at reliable conclusions on future trends in travel behavior. To aim to find how demographic change will influence the tourism market and how the industry can adapt to those changes. The travel analysis provided data on tourism consumer behavior, including attitudes, motives and intentions. Since, 1970 year, it is based on a random sample, representative for the population in private households aged 14 years or older. Then, a continuous high scientific standard combined with a national and international users makes the travel analysis a useful tool and reliable source for tourism industry and policy decisions. It aimed to gather statistical data. e.g. on the age structure and on demographic trends, quantitative and qualitative analysis with time series data from the travel analysis. It shows e.g. not only the future volume , quite different from today's seniors, or how who will travel of family holidays will change, e.g. single parents of low, but grandparents of growing significance for tourism.

Demographic change is said to be one of the important drivers for new trends in consumer traveling change behavior in most European countries (e.g. Lind 2001). Because the growing number of senior citizens in the European Union and other industrialized countries, such as the USA and Japan, looks to become one of the major marketing challenges for the tourism industry. United Nations statistics predict that the share of people being 60 age or older will grow dramatically in the coming future, and is expected to rise from 10 percent of the world population in 2000 year to more than 20 percent in 2050 year (United Nations Population Division, 2001). From its statistic, some data showed that travel propensity increased throughout life until the age of about 50 years of age and was then kept stable until very late in life 75 age. The most important results is that the travel propensity when getting older is not going down between 65 and 75 age of course, the overall development of this variable is influenced by a lot of other factors which are responsible for quite a variation over time. It is now possible to suggest that the general pattern of travel propensity is one of the key indicators for holiday life cycle travel behavior, includes three stages. The growth stage tends to increase from early adult hood until 45 age old or when reaching some 80%. The next stage is stabilization from the ages of around 50 age, until 75 age old, starting with a lower increase. Finally, the decrease stage is a slight decrease occurs once people reach the more advanced age of 75 age to 85 age old (Lohmann &

Danielsson 2001).

So, it seems Germany government tourism prediction to future travelers' behavior indicated these findings, such as on how future senior generations will travel, who had used survey data to examine the patterns of travel behavior of a generation getting older and applied the findings to draw conclusions on the future. Also, it predicted that on the future of family trips, family segmentation will be the travel behavior patterns in the future. These findings together with the statistical data on demographic change allowed for a better understanding of the coming tends in family holidays. It's aim developed in consumer behavior related to demographic change and predicted what will happen future of tourism one had to consider other influences and drivers as well, for example, trends on the supply side. e.g. low cost airlines or in travelling consumption behavior in general whether how the past may provide a key to predict travel patterns of senior citizens to the future.

Given the projected growth of the senior citizens market, designing specific marketing strategies to meet the prospective needs of elderly tourists will become increasingly important. It has been an implicit assumption that it will be a close relationship between the travel behavior of today's senior citizens and the those of future ones. The growing number of senior citizens in the world. e.g. China, Hong Kong, Japan, USA etc. countries. Global senior citizen tourism market will be based solely on demographic predictions about the future of the population's age structure. However, many of these seniors won't only live longer but will be fitter and more active until later in life. Many of the will also have plenty in life. Many of them will also have plenty of time and money to spend on travel. So, will these new seniors behave like today's senior citizens? Will they adopt the same travel behavior as the previous generation or become a new market of oldies for the leisure and tourism industry? However, to determine the actual number of senior citizens who will be travelling and to sought to evaluate and specify certain difficult to predict the actual numbers of senior citizen to any country. However, they can be based on the implicit assumption that there is a close relationship between the travel behavior of past, present and future seniors. But is this a valid assumption? As the revise- analysis travel analysis survey, which was conducted in Germany every year, offered some interesting data possibilities. It was designed to monitor the holiday travel behavior, opinions and attitudes of Germans and has been carried out since 1970 year, questions in the questionnaire. Data are based on face to face interviews, with a representative sample of more than 7,500 respondents, the interviews being carried out in January each year. All results refer to the average for the defined generated, which ranges generally over ten years. The group of people then at the age of 60 to 69 age is described. This corresponds to the same generation ten years ago, when they had an age of 50 to 59 age. When this methodological approach is not necessarily very sophisticated, it does have the important advantages of being cost effective.

Q36 IS (AI) big data gathering method a better psychological method to compare human marketing research method predict travel behavioral consumption?

On the psychological view point, I think individual traveler's character will have those kind of personal characteristics. First, simplicity searchers value above everything ease not transparency in their travel planning and holiday making, and are willing to avoid having to go through extensive research. Second, cultural purists use their travel as an opportunity to immerse themselves in an unfamiliar looking to break themselves entirely from their home lives and engage. Sincerely with a different way of living. Third, social capital seekers understand that to be well travelled is a personal quality, and their choices are shaped by their desire to take maximum of social reward from their travel. They will exploit the potential of digital media to enrich and inform their experiences, and structure their adventures always keeping in mind they are being watched by online audiences. Finally, reward hunters seek a return on the investment who make in their busy , high-achieving lives. Linked in part to the growing trend of wellness, including both physical and mental self-improvement who seek truly extraordinary and often indulgent or luxurious' must have experiences.

Why needs to know the personal character of individual traveler's characteristics? Because if travel agents could feel which kinds of individual traveler's character, then who can predict which kind of travel package to design to them more easily. For example, how to determine future travel behavior from past travel experience and perceptions of risk and safety? We need to concern that the influences of past international travel experience, types of risk associated with international travel and the overall degree of safety feeling during international travel on individual's travelling experiences likelihood of travelling to various geographic regions on their next international vacation trip or avoidance of those regions, due to perceived risk. Because individual traveler's experience of safety risk degree to the countries, it will influence who chooses to go to the countries/country to travel again.

Why travelers avoid certain destinations are as relevant decision making as why who choose to go to the country(countries) to travel. Perceptions of risk and safety and travel experiences are likely to influence travel decisions; efforts to predict future travel behavior can benefit to individual tourist's decision making.

As Weber & Bottom (1989) defined risky decision is as "choices among alternatives that can be described by probability distributions over possible outcomes" (p.114). Some psychologists judge subjective perceptions of physical reality, i.e. image of a particular tourist destination, whereas value judgement refers to the way individual rank destinations according to whose attributes. i.e. attractiveness, safety, risk etc. factors to form on overall image. So, if the individual traveler had unhappy and worried and unsafe experiences to go to where the place(country) to travel during whose vacation time before. Then, this negative travel experience will influence who is afraid to go to the place (country) to travel again. Risk of place, country, destination or region means the danger is relatively high to the place, i.e. increasing in airplane accidents, crime or terrorist activity targeting citizens of potential traveler's nationality or the probability of occurrence is great , i.e. recent occurrences involving travel regions/destinations under consideration or effective actions to control consequences exist. i.e. selecting safe regions and destinations, taking extra precautions when traveling to risky destinations. These risk factors will influence the individual traveler who chooses to cancel travel plan to go to the country again.

Another interesting research, how to predict behavioral intention of choosing a travel destination, which has focus of tourism research for years, but the complex decision making process leading to the choice of a travel destination has not been well researched. The planned behavior model using its core constructs, attitude, subjective norm and perceived behavioral control, with the addition of the past behavioral variable on behavioral intention of choosing a travel destination.

Understanding why people travel and what factors influence their behavioral intention of choosing a travel destination is beneficial to tourism planning and marketing. Understanding travel motivation is the push and pull model. The idea of the push and pull model is the decomposition of an individual's choice of a travel destination into two forces. The first force is the push factor that pushes an individual away home and attempts to develop a general desire to go somewhere else, without specifying where that may be. The second force is the pull factor, that pulls on individual toward a destination, due to a region specific travel location or perceived attractiveness of a destination. The respective push and pull factors illustrate that people travel because who are pushed by their internal motives and pulled by external forces of a destination. Nevertheless, how push and pull factors guide people's attitude and how these attributes lead to behavioral intentions of choosing a travel destination have rarely been investigated. The decision making process leading to the choice of a travel destination is a very complex process. The planned behavior model is as a research framework to predict the behavioral intention of choosing a travel destination. The model based on the three constructs of attitude, subjective norm, and perceived behavioral control (Fishbein & Ajzen, 1975).

In conclusion, the factors can influence travelers who decide to choose to travel the country, which include personal safety was perceived to the highest motivation factors among the important factors which include, scenic beauty, cultural interests, friendliness of local people, price of trip, services in hotels and restaurants, quality and variety of food and shopping facilities and services. The factors include both push and pull. Push factors include knowledge, prestige, and enhancement of human relationship etc., whereas, the most significant pull factors include high technologic image, expenditure and accessibility etc. For example, Japanese travelers visiting Hong Kong. Push factors are such as exploration dream fulfillment and pull factors are such as benefits sought, attractions and good climate city. It will be the factor of future travel patterns and motivations of sub-cultural and ethic groups for Japanese choice to go to Hong Kong travelling.

Q 37 How can apply (AI) digital channel (big data gathering method) predict travelling consumer behaviors?

(AI) big data digital channel can be applied to help travelling businesses to evaluate whether how much the e-ticket price and travelling package price is the most attractive or reasonable to persuade travelling consumers feel it is the most reasonable price to choose to buy the airline's e-tickets or the travel agent's travelling package product from internet channel . It helps travelling consumers to feel which airlines or travelling agents which ought change their e-ticket and/or travelling package price to let travelling consumers to choose to buy the airline e-ticket or the travelling agent's travelling package products from internet channel. It can be applied to predict whether how many travelling consumer numbers can be increased or decreased when the airline e-ticket price is variable or the travelling agent travelling package price is variable . It aims to give opinions to help any online airlines or travelling agents to judge whether which e-ticket or travelling package price is the most reasonable to let travelling consumers to accept to choose to buy which airline's e-tickets or traveling agent's package products more attractive.

Thus, (AI) e-ticket or e-travelling package price measurement technology can be preference to be applied online communication ecommerce and mobile phone internet platform aspect. As traveling businesses can enter their past e-ticket or travelling package prices data and past travelling customer number data into computer or mobile. Then, (AI) price measurement technology can gather these data to analyze these e-ticket or travelling package product prices and past travelling customer number to compare their e-ticket and/or travelling package prices variable changing range level to find their e-ticket and /or travelling package price variable difference to measure to make conclusion about every travelling package or/and e-ticket product's price variable changing will influence how many travelling customer number increase or decrease changing to choose to sell their different kinds of travelling package or e-ticket products more accurate. Then, (AI) price measurement software will help them to analyze all past e-ticket and/or travelling package price variable changing data to compare whether which e-ticket and/or travelling package price range can let travelling customers to feel it is more reasonable and attractive to influence them to choose to buy their e-ticket or travelling package product among different airlines and travel agent choices. Because any e-ticket or travelling package product's price is one important factor to influence travelling consumers to choose to buy the airline's e-tickets or travelling agent's travelling package products.

For example, Amazon publish has applied (AI) price measurement technology to help authors to decide how much every different topic of e-book or paper book price, it can attract the largest number of readers to buy. Any one author only needs to type whose book name to Amazon publish author himself/herself Amazon website. Amazon publish (AI) price measurement learning machine will help them to auto-calculate and judge how much e-book or paper book price is the most attractive and the most reasonable in order to increase reader number to buy their e-books or paper books to read. So, (AI) online price measurement machine will gather past similar book names and past every similar book readers' reading times and the number of readers to give opinions to let every author to judge whether his/her very new e-book or paper book ought charge how much price to the e-book or paper book which can attract many readers to choose to buy. Although, it is not ensure that the e-book or paper book price must let readers to feel it is the most reasonable price to choose to buy in reader's view point. However, it has other factors to influence readers' choice to buy the e-book or paper book, e.g. whether the book content is attractive to public, the author's familiarity, the book's page is enough or not to satisfy readers to read etc. factors. But, instead of all these extra factors to influence readers to choose to buy the book to read. (AI) price measurement learning machine can real give opinions to every author to let them to judge the e-book or paper book different price range whether is too high to influence readers to choose to buy to read or tool low to influence readers feel it is possible poor content book to compare other similar content books. Thus, (AI) price measurement machine can help authors to predict every reader's reading behaviors or reading experience and reading habit from online channel in short time easily. The author only enter the book name to let Amazon publish price measurement machine to check, it will follow past reader's reading habit and reading experience to judge whether the similar all book topic sale record to judge how much price is the reasonable price to attract many readers to buy the book.

Hence, (AI) can be applied to digital channel to help travelling businesses to predict travelling consumer behavior in the future. In the future, mobile/smartphone, laptop, desktop will be most frequent used ecommerce channels to develop online business. So, (AI) can be also applied to these platforms to gather data to make analysis to help travelling businesses to predict travelling consumer purchase behaviors popularly. Due to , ecommerce is popular to global, so digital online and instore channels can be one good channel to let (AI) learning machine to make platform to gather past every online travelling consumer purchase (buying) experience data to help travelling businesses to build airline or travelling agent brand personality and having a responsible, positive impact on society.

To apply (AI) learning machine technology to understand travelling customer online purchase behavior, it will raise business e-commerce successful chance: For example, (AI) learning machine can help travelling businesses to gather data to analyze to determine whether short-term or long-term signals in the online travelling consumer behavior that indicate higher purchase intents to let every online travelling business to know. (AI) learning machine can find that online users with long-term purchasing intent tend to save and click through on more content.

However, as online travelling users approach the time of purchase their activity becomes more topically focused and actions shift from saves to searches from online travelling consumption channel. Then, (AI) learning machine will further find that the brand airline and/or travelling agent purchase signals in online travelling consumption behavior can exist weakness before an online travelling purchase is made and can also be traced across different online travelling purchase categories. Finally, (AI) learning machine synthesize these insights in predictive models of online travelling user purchasing intent to the brand of airline or/and travelling agent travelling package product. Taken together, it's work identifies a set of general principles and signals that can be used to model online travelling user e-ticket and/or travelling package purchasing intent across many online content discovery applications. Thus, (AI) learning machine can help online travelling businesses to gather any online travelling users' click online travelling behaviors data to judge whether there are how many online travelling users will choose to find their online travelling business websites to make final decisions to buy their travelling package or/and e-ticket products from online channels. Then, it will give opinions to help the online travelling businesses to let it to judge whether what are the important website factors will help its online travelling business to attract many online travelling consumers, e.g. designing unattractive travelling website issue, online unattractive scene photos issue, unclear website travelling photo color issue, unclear website travelling advertisement message, contents and words impressions issue, lacking image movement frequent attractive seeing issue etc. different website factors. Thus, online digital channel will be one good choice to apply (AI) learning machine to help travelling businesses to predict travelling consumer behaviors.

Thus, (AI) big data technology can also assist travelling consumers to gather different manufacturers' data to compare what their advantages and disadvantages of their travelling package products are. Then, travelling consumers can make comparison to choose which airline or travelling agent is the suitable to whom to buy e-ticket or pre-booking travelling package in online travelling consumption market.

.

Thus, I believe that artificial intelligent "big data" gathering method can be suggested to be applied to attempt to predict travelling consumer behavioral changes in global online travelling business environment, the reasons are as below:
On the travelling consumer's beneficial hand, travelling consumers can apply this (AI) big data gathering method to attempt to gather any global airline e-tickets and/or travelling agent's package product data to be analyzed by this artificial intelligent learning system to compare human general marketing research method, e.g. survey, questionnaire, marketing plan etc. different human judgement methods to predict traveler consumption behavioral change model. Then, it analyzed all the different data to compare what are the range of the most reasonable e-ticket and/or travelling package online purchase history and sale in order to make more accurate prediction to future traveler change traveling consumption behavioral model in next month, or next half year or next year short

term period traveling consumption change prediction.

Reference

Backman and others "motivation is conceptually viewed as " a state of need, a condition that services as a driving force to display different kind of behavior toward certain types of activities, developing preferences, arriving at some expected satisfactory outcome.", 1995, p.15.

Fishbein & Ajzen, "The model based on the three constructs of attitude, subjective norm, and perceived behavioral control". 1975.

Hsu et al. "A tourist behavior model has been developed, called the expectation, motivation and attitude " (EMA) model ,2010.

ICT,WWW . "Switzerland has one of the highest population-to-computer ratio in Europe." Switzerland, 2005.

Jorea Ministry of Environment, " For South Korea environmental attitude is a major factor in decision making vis-a-vis the consumption of " green" food and services", Korea, 2015.

Korea Ministry Of Environment. Public Organizations spend 2.2 Trillon Korean Won To
Purchase green Products in 2014; Ministry Of Environment: Sejoung, Korea, 2015.

Lind , Lohmann & Danielsson , United Nations Population Division, "Demographic change is said to be one of the important drivers for new trends in consumer traveling change behavior in most European countries". 2001.

Mayne, Lonnie. " Evolve of die in the age of the consumer". Entrepreneur, N.P. , 16 Apr. 2014. web of Oct. 2016.

Lee, D.; Kim, M. ; Lee, J. adoption of green electricity policies: Investigating the role of environmental attitudes via big data-driven search-queries. Energy policy 2016. 90, 187-201.

Lee, Terrence, " Tech in Asia-connecting Asia's startup system " Tech. in Asia- connecting Asia's startup ecosystem, N.p.,4 July 2016.

Weber & Bottorn "risky decision is as choices among alternatives that can be described by probability distributions over possible outcomes" , 1989, p.114.